PRAISE FOR *BRICK BY BRICK*

'Don't mentor one more person, don't lead one more coaching session, don't conduct one more appraisal, without having first read this book. Paul Bassi reviews success, breaks it down, pulverises it . . . and then rebuilds it in a way that forces readers to ask questions of themselves: excellent!'

LORD DIGBY JONES, *International businessman and cross-bench peer in the House of Lords*

'Paul's energising argument is that anyone can be a success in life. Whilst there is no entitlement or magic ingredient, Paul offers practical advice built on his years of experience in the property industry. Always a modest man, his tips are generously given and sound so natural. The tough bit will be following them!'

ANDY STREET CBE, *Mayor of West Midlands and former MD of John Lewis*

'Through his philanthropic work, Paul has shared his success with his friends, neighbours and local community. He has a generous spirit and believes that everyone – no matter where they come from – should be able to succeed as far as their individual talent and hard work can take them. He is an inspiration to us all.'

TOM WATSON MP, *Deputy Leader of the Labour Party*

'Whoever and wherever we are, the "bottom line" is that we all need a beckoning vision, a life plan or aspiration that pulls us on and drives us on. Nobody is better able to picture that vision for us, and ground it in reality, than Paul Bassi.'

JOHN CRABTREE OBE, *Lord Lieutenant of the West Midlands*

'Paul unpacks what many people want to know in a simple, accessible and human way. His words and actions have inspired me, whether he is in front of me talking over a cup of tea, or whilst I am having one of my "what would Paul do here?" conversations with myself. I would compel anyone of any age and walk of life to read this book, as there will be something inside it that will resonate with you.'

PAUL THANDI DL, *CEO, The NEC Group*

'Paul has been immensely successful, achieved by deploying his most powerful weapons – good old-fashioned common sense and a straightforward way of dealing with people and business. Combined with a fabulous work ethic, he has become the go-to businessman in the Midlands.'

WILLIAM WYATT, *CEO, Caledonia Investments Plc*

'The journey of Paul's family as Indian immigrants, through to Paul achieving huge success across his businesses in the United Kingdom, is a truly inspirational read'.

ASHA BHOSLE, *Legendary singer and global restaurateur*

BRICK BY BRICK

BRICK BY BRICK

Success in Business and Life

PAUL BASSI CBE

BLOOMSBURY BUSINESS

LONDON • NEW YORK • OXFORD • NEW DELHI • SYDNEY

BLOOMSBURY BUSINESS
Bloomsbury Publishing Plc
50 Bedford Square, London, WC1B 3DP, UK
1385 Broadway, New York, NY 10018, USA

BLOOMSBURY, BLOOMSBURY BUSINESS and the Diana logo are
trademarks of Bloomsbury Publishing Plc

First published in Great Britain 2019

10 9 8 7 6 5 4 3 2

Cover design by Steve Leard

A catalogue record for this book is available from the British Library.

A catalog record for this book is available from the Library of Congress.

ISBN: HB: 978-1-4729-7222-4
       ePDF: 978-1-4729-7219-4
       eBook: 978-1-4729-7220-0

Typeset by RefineCatch Limited, Bungay, Suffolk
Printed and bound in Great Britain

To find out more about our authors and books visit www.bloomsbury.com
and sign up for our newsletters.

All profits generated from the sale of this book that are due to the author, Paul Bassi CBE, will be donated to The Bond Wolfe Charitable Trust (Charity No 1132430)

CONTENTS

ACKNOWLEDGEMENTS

Thank you to . . .

My faith in Sikhism

My faith in Sikhism as a philosophy of life and our one god for the blessing, health and good fortune that has been bestowed on me and my family and friends.

Bhagat Singh Bassi

My grandfather. Without his courage to take those first steps from our village in Punjab, full of hope and fear in equal proportion, my journey and adventure would not have happened. Our family will forever be indebted.

My children

My beautiful eldest daughter Terri, you were the first in our family to graduate from university with a Masters degree. You have matured into a caring and responsible young lady, and wife. To my son-in-law, Amo, for the respect and love you have shown my daughter and the rest of the family. I am proud of you both and wish you well in your married life ahead.

My son, Bobby. You are growing into a highly respected young man and exceptional company executive. Having put the necessary hard work into your career, coupled with the dedication and commitment to all you do, will give you the golden future that your old head teacher said you would have. Thank you for your loyalty, support and your understanding.

My radiant youngest daughter Nikita, aka 'the Indian'. You are talented, caring and loving, whilst being determined and loyal to all those with whom you share your life , especially your charming young man Nicholas. Don't change – and believe in yourself. Enjoy your life; you are a very special young lady.

My wonderful nephews

My favourite eldest nephew Gurpreet, your leadership as the eldest of the next generation is the foundation of the future. You are an outstanding young man and husband to the beautiful Karen and a fantastic dad to young Dylan ('smiler'). You have an amazing career ahead of you, enjoy the journey.

My favourite middle nephew, and my namesake, Paul, aka 'totters'. You are a gifted young man and the world is your playground. Remember, there are no limits – and glass ceilings don't exist. You are going to have an outstanding career and it is thoroughly deserved. No matter where you go, don't forget to give your old uncle a call once a week.

My favourite youngest nephew, George, aka 'horse'. The baby of the family is turning into a very capable young man. Your gentle nature and caring personality are recognized by all. You can be and do whatever you want to and I am confident that you have a great future ahead of you.

Mum and Dad

The values and morals passed down to the future generations of honesty, hard work and commitment are the greatest legacy one can bequeath. You gave me the philosophy of always 'doing the right thing', the bedrock of all that I have done and will do.

My brothers and sisters

Thank you Kamaljit, Rashpal, Dharminder and Baljinder for your support and loyalty. It's been a great adventure and now we watch our children with pride, enjoying seeing them progress with their adventures.

My in-laws – Paul, Pam, Sheila and Bill

For your guidance and support and for the integrity you have imbedded in your children and grandchildren.

My boys /oppos!

My close friends, many of you whom I have known for decades, you give me balance and total support and of course make me laugh and even laugh at my jokes. You are always there in good times and sometimes sad times.

Nick Baird, Mark Bevan, Nick Billig, Patrice Boilletot, Richard Boot OBE, Tony Brewer, Stuart Burkin, Eric Jones, Hreesh Kenth, Pawan Kenth, Peter Knowles, Ian Livingstone, Peter London, Afsal Majid, Khalid Minhas, Amir Mosavian, David Myers, Harry Parmar, Adrian Pegler, Alan 'Fonzy' Prince, Andy Savage, Stuart Shields, Gurpal Showker, Jag Shoker, Andrew 'Tiger' Simpson, Ash Sudera, Andy Szwed and Simon Webb.

My 'girlfriends'

Jo Ball, Sandra Boot, Linda Daly, Suman Hollier, Lynn Jones, Denny Knowles, Denise Law, Judy London, Jan Morrell, Lesley Myers, Karen Parmar, Debbie Pegler, Tracey Prince, Kay Savage, Helen Shields, Sue Simpson, Maree Smith, Chris Szwed, Sally Tucker and Alison Webb. These ladies have been great friends for decades. You do make me laugh and sometimes make me pull my hair out. Thank you for all the good times and for looking after my mates.

My godchildren

Oliver, Morgan, Ewan and Luke. It's an honour and very humbling to be asked to be your godfather. You all have great parents and I am sure you will all make them proud and grow up to fulfil your enormous potential.

Project 'Brick by Brick'

Josh Davis, James Lumsden-Cook, Vafa Payman, Ian Hallsworth, Rachel Nicholson, Tony Mulliken, Amelia Knight, Ben McCluskey and the rest of the teams at Bloomsbury and Midas. Without your skill and professionalism this project would never have got off the ground. Thank you for your support and confidence in me.

My heroes

My grandmothers, Gurdev Kaur Bassi, Pritam Kaur Chaudri and Aunty Surjit Kaur. These ladies were the backbone of all that has happened: their courage, work ethic and sheer determination were incredible. They overcame all the odds to allow the rest of us to have the lives and great futures we enjoy today.

The great and the good

Birmingham and the wider Midlands is going through a positive period of economic, social and cultural rebirth and I believe it will become a global city and region of the future. This is only possible due to the work and dedication of many great people. In particular, I would like to thank the following for their contribution to my city and region:

the late Rod Ackrill,

Ron Atkinson,

Dr Nasir Awan MBE DL,

Anita Bhalla OBE,

the late Lord Bhattacharyya,

Saqib Bhatti,

Jerry Blackett,

Richard Boot OBE,

Ranjit Boparan,

Sir Albert Bore,

Dame Christine Braddock DBE,

Keith Bradshaw and family,

Phil Carlin,

Alan Chatham,

John Crabtree OBE,

David Davies OBE,

the late Roger Dickens CBE,

Steve Dodd,

Lord Bob Edmiston,

the late Sir Doug Ellis OBE,

Paul Faulkner,

Tony Gallagher,

Stuart Griffiths OBE,

the late David Grove OBE,

Mim Hall,

Byron Head,

the Horton family,

Glenn Howells,

Alan Hudson,

Alan Jackson,

Ninder Johal DL,

Lord Digby Jones and Lady Pat Jones,

Manjit Kang,

Arnie Kaplan MBE,

Preet Kaur Gill MP,

Paul Kehoe CBE,

Jaswinder Singh Khatkar,

Jindy Khaira.

Dame Julia King DBE,

Greg Lawson,

the late Peter Mawdsley,

Anthony McCourt,

Katie McPhilimey,

Nicola Fleet-Milne,

Rupert Mucklow and family,

Tommy Nagra,

Waheed Nazir,

Tim Pile,

Dr Aman Puri,

Neil Rami,

Roy Richardson and family,

Sir Peter Rigby DL,

Dr. Paul Sabapathy CVO CBE,

Perm Saini,

Jas Sansi,

the Shipley family,

Graham Silk,

Charan Singh,

Shailesh Solanki,

Andy Street CBE,

Gary Taylor,

Paul Thandi DL,

Geoff Thomas,

Simon Topman MBE,

Stewart Towe CBE,

Jonnie Turpie MBE,

David Urquhart,

Geoff Walker,

Mike Ward,

Bob Warman,

Tom Watson MP,

Tim Watts DL,

Jason Wouhra OBE,

and Tony Deep Wouhra MBE.

My team

Everything we have achieved has only been possible due to the commitment of some key individuals in our business. Without these people, we would not be where we are today. *'Alone we go nowhere, together we go further.'* Thank you all for the trust and confidence you have placed in me – and see you tomorrow morning! Thanks to:

Katie Bolton,

Kate Campbell,

Hayley Chambers,

Ian Clark,

Perm Daley,

Ron Darlington,

Anna Durnford,

Nouman Farooqui,

Catherine Gee,

Jaimon George,

Richard Horwell,

Sunil Kumar,

Charlie London,

James Mattin,

Donna Mooney,

Dominic Norunha,

Andrew Osborne,

Sue Randell,

Jody Sargeant

Jack Sears,
Ian Tudor,
David Waldron,
Paul Warder,
and Lisa Worrall

My advisers and supporters

Good advisers are worth their weight in gold and we have been fortunate
to have encountered and engaged with some brilliant ones. Some of you
have been there to support us on a daily basis and others have allowed
our business to make quantum leaps over the last thirty-five years. Your
trust, confidence and belief in us is humbling. Thanks to:

Azhic Basirov,
Stephen Benson,
Anand Bhosle,
Asha Bhosle,
Paul Cliff,
Tim Cockcroft,
John Crabtree,
John Duckers,
Trevor Foster,
Susheel Gupta,
Ashley Hudson,
Neil Hutchinson,
David Jones,
Baldev Kang,
Stephen Karle,

Peter London,

Harj Millington

Nick Moxon,

Jim O'Donnell,

Jacko Page,

David Parsons,

Ruth Pipkin,

Sue Potter,

Jamie Richards,

Tim Robertson,

Andy Skinner,

Steve Skinner,

Rob Thompson,

Craig Upton,

Paul Wedge,

and William Wyatt.

Special thanks to . . .

Rory and Marcus Daly for your undoubted friendship and support. It's been an adventure and a pleasure to have built our businesses together and watched our families grow. Of course, it's not over, there's lots more to do and it's also time to enjoy the fruits of our labour!

My Lieutenant

My longstanding, loyal, trusted, dedicated and highly talented Lieutenant, Anna Durnford, I would be lost without you!

My wife Priya

I have been extremely fortunate to be married to you and have you as my partner: spending my life with you, a beautiful woman, a good friend, great mother, daughter and sister and an awesome wife and best friend. There is no doubt that alongside a good man is a great woman. I look forward to the adventure ahead, growing old and becoming glamparents and great-glamparents!

Paul Bassi

Introduction

Success is a simple thing that most people believe to be complicated. We look up to people at the peak of their professions and believe they must be incredible and rare talents. But it isn't true. In the vast majority of cases, the people at the top have got there by following disciplines that are open to everyone. Their success is far more normal, and achievable, than is generally understood. I believe in God-given talent, but I also think everyone has the God-given right to be successful. This book has been written to show you how to achieve just that.

Normality isn't something people usually associate with success: in life, business or property. But success is normal, even natural, and it should be seen as just that. Too many people get told that their goals are out of reach and they should give up or compromise on them. Unfortunately, plenty of them take this message to heart.

People have a lot of mistaken ideas about success. Some lack confidence and believe they don't have it in them to be successful, thinking they are not worthy or that success is somebody else's domain. Others, with the opposite problem, think they can get away without putting the work in and don't bother to lay proper foundations. For very different reasons, both are wrong. As Henry

Ford famously said, **'Whether you think you can, or you think you can't, you're right.'**

More people should know the reality about success, which is that it's closer than you think, but harder work than you expect. It's neither the impossibility that some claim, nor the get-rich-quick fantasy peddled by others.

You will be successful in life – by your own definition, which is the only one that matters – if you set yourself a central ambition and follow some fundamental principles about how to achieve it, many of which can be learned by studying other successful people. The advice in this book is primarily focused on business and property, my areas of expertise, but much of it is applicable whatever life and career you want to pursue. It's about how you can organize your life around a guiding purpose – what I call the 'big picture': set goals that are rigorous enough that you won't give up on them; and then build a business that will underpin your success and that of your family and your team for the long term. It is about the relentless approach needed in all aspects of work and life to achieve success.

I don't view my own career as exceptional, or my own talents as out of the ordinary, so the advice here is not complex or difficult to grasp. It is straightforward, but has the virtue of having been tested over my thirty-five-year career, as the son of immigrants who arrived with almost nothing, to becoming one of the most prominent property investors in the Midlands. I currently lead a property and business portfolio of over £300m that has managed real estate worth more than £5bn on behalf of clients, with annual sales of over £200m.

I tell my own story in the opening chapter, before going on to outline my philosophy of success, what I've learned from other successful people, how you can plan your own journey to success, followed by the principles of building a successful business and a thriving property portfolio. The intention is to provide a roadmap that can allow anyone to be successful and, most importantly, fulfilled in life.

The advice that follows is both what I've learned from experience building those businesses, and investing in those properties, and also what I have learned by observing and working alongside those with much bigger companies and deeper pockets than me.

There are many different advice points which cover the ins and outs of how you can set goals for yourself, go about building a business and learn to invest well in property. But above all I will be saying two things.

The first is that you need to establish a big picture if you want to succeed. Unless you have an overall vision – something that the career you pursue, and the businesses you may build, contribute towards – you will struggle to find the motivation and stamina required to stay the course. As I will explain, visualizing the end game is about the context of your own life, not what others want or expect from you. Forget other people's benchmarks: find something that excites, challenges and scares you, a big picture that is worth living and working hard for.

The counterbalance to setting your goals and your sights high is that you will have to work relentlessly to achieve those ambitions. Whether you're building a business or a career, it needs to be based on firm foundations: a network and market intelligence, the desire to get to know everything and everyone in the professional village you have chosen. If you're not prepared to put in this spadework, then you can forget about achieving success on a meaningful, long-term and sustainable level.

Don't believe anyone who tells you there are shortcuts and easy paths to being successful. I've seen countless people attempt this road, and every single one finishes in a dead end and with the regret of unfulfilled potential. There is no short cut to achieving your big picture: you either invest the time and effort in building your knowledge, reputation and network over many years, or you don't achieve your goals. It's that simple.

I knew almost none of this when I started my career, at the age of eighteen, as the first in my family to wear a shirt and tie to work; or when I launched my first business a handful of years later. From my parents, and through working in the corner shop they owned, I learned the importance of hard work. My career has also been influenced by the Sikh values my grandmother taught me: respect, honesty, never fearing anyone or wanting to be feared, and sharing the proceeds of your work with others.

The rest I have had to pick up along the way, throwing myself into an industry I knew very little about, and finding people I could learn from. I hope that by putting everything I now know about building success in one place, I can help save you some of the trouble, and make you realize that success can be your destiny too.

The advice in this book applies to a wide range of people. It doesn't matter if you are right at the beginning of your career, or well advanced in it and pondering a change of course. You might be thinking about investing a bit of spare capital in property, or starting a full-time career as a professional investor.

What I've found out, from getting a tiny overdraft from a local bank, and investing tens of thousands in residential properties in the 1980s, to the last decade or so of my career, raising over £100m from institutional investors and building a portfolio worth hundreds of millions, is that the same principles apply however small or large the deal. Even if you are just dipping your toe into the water, it needs to be done with much of the same care and rigour as the professionals. And while it might be your big picture to build a small but perfectly formed business, that doesn't make it any less of a precise and exacting art than trying to create a public company or a multinational. I believe that the principles I outline here will be relevant to those building companies and property portfolios of all shapes and sizes, and indeed to those whose ambitions lie beyond business.

Above all, I want people reading this to understand that no one else has the right to tell you what you should be aspiring to, or to set limits on your ambitions. Success is normal, making money is achievable and fulfilling your dreams is doable. It won't be easy, it won't happen quickly (because overnight success takes fifteen years) and it won't come without making sacrifices, but it is all eminently possible, if you want it enough and are prepared to be disciplined and relentless in your approach. This book will show you what it takes.

1

Punjab to the Palace

The true meaning of life is to plant trees, under whose shade you do not expect to sit.

NELSON HENDERSON

In every personal and family history there are defining journeys. For me there were two, about six decades apart, that bookend my life so far and help explain it.

The first took place seven years before I was born. In 1955 my grandfather, Bhagat Singh Bassi, and his brother Jagat Singh took themselves to the visa office in Jalandhar, Punjab. They wanted to get out of India, like many of their generation who planned to earn some money abroad and then return home. At that time, India had not long achieved its independence and was still dealing with the turmoil left behind by British colonial rule. People like my grandfather faced a struggle to improve their lives and enjoy any prosperity.

The brothers were twins, who farmed a small ancestral piece of land, but the journey they were about to undertake would separate them forever. Bhagat got a visa to come to the UK. Jagat's destination was Argentina. After getting on their respective planes, they never saw each other again. My grandfather left behind his young wife and five children, including the eldest, my father, Santokh.

Fast forward to the spring of 2010 and I was with my family at our house in Marbella. In a few days I was due at Buckingham Palace to collect my CBE. Then the Icelandic ash cloud descended, planes were grounded and it looked like we would be stranded. But it's not really an option to phone up the Queen and say you're going to come another day. So, a driver and people carrier were hired and with my wife Priya, son Bobby, daughter Nikita and nephew Paul, along with two of Nikita's friends, Ciara and Fran, we were driven from Marbella to London via Paris. We arrived the night before the ceremony and I attended in a suit specially purchased to avoid meeting Prince Charles in my shorts and sandals.

In two generations, my family story has evolved from Punjabi immigrants arriving with almost nothing, to being honoured among the great and good at a royal palace. I can hardly imagine what my grandfather would have thought had he been told back in the mid-1950s that his trip to the visa office would eventually lead to a ceremony in the state rooms of Buckingham Palace. But, as distant in time and place as the two events might be, they are connected in important ways. You need the one to explain the other. Everything in my life has ultimately followed from my grandfather's decision to get on a plane and leave his homeland behind, in search of prosperity for his family: his big picture.

My own story really begins with the arrival of my father in the UK in 1957, aged sixteen, now able to work and hoping to send money back home for the rest of the family. He arrived at a time when the UK desperately needed immigrant labour to rebuild its battered post-war economy, with rationing having ended only three years earlier. In India we were a family of agricultural landowners, from the Jat Sikh community. But when my dad came to England he had the equivalent of just £2 in his pocket. With my grandfather, he found work wherever he could in factories and foundries, all across the Midlands from Birmingham to the Black Country and Derby and further north in Huddersfield.

This was a very different era of industrial relations. All the South Asians looking for work would crowd outside the factory gates every morning, and the foreman would come out and pull in only as many as he needed for that day. If you wanted to work, you had to fight your way to the front of the scrum, or you weren't getting paid that day. Eventually, my dad and grandfather earned enough to move the rest of the family to the UK.

In 1960 my parents were married. Two years later I was born at what was Dudley Road Hospital, now City Hospital Birmingham. It was an arranged marriage, not in the kind of stately home surroundings that my eldest daughter recently enjoyed at her wedding, but in the back garden of my nan's terrace in Southall, in front of just two dozen guests. My parents, like their own, had migrated from Birmingham to London in search of better prospects and to fulfil their big picture for themselves and their young family.

Getting down to work

From a very early age, due to the Sikh work ethic instilled in me by my family, I was working. It never occurred to me that it should be any other way: there was work to be done, money was valued and always respected, and I had to contribute. From the age of six or seven I would help out my mum with the jobs she did at home: garment sewing throughout the year, paid piecemeal, and making crackers before Christmas.

Like most immigrants, my dad would work as many jobs as he could to make money and get by. He'd work all day in the family corner shop, do a factory shift at night and, in what little spare time remained, give driving lessons. I remember being confused that his car, a sky-blue Vauxhall Viva, wasn't parked outside our front door on Southall's Park Avenue, but down at the end of the road. It was only later that I learned this was because it had run out of petrol. Every penny was being counted, and there wasn't always money to fill up the car, pay the mortgage and put food on the table at the same time.

By this point our small terrace was providing a home for an extended family that comprised me, my parents, sister Rashpal and brother Kamal, my grandmother and my father's youngest sister, whom he had taken responsibility for looking after. Our house was small as it was, but we only occupied the downstairs: my parents and Kamal sleeping in the front room and the rest of us at the back, which doubled up as a bedroom by night and a dining room and lounge by day. This allowed my parents to take in lodgers upstairs, another way of earning some extra cash.

By watching every penny and saving scrupulously, my parents had secured a mortgage and been able to afford the Park Avenue house, from which point they slowly started climbing the property ladder. Except their approach wasn't to use the capital earned from flipping houses as an opportunity to improve our standard of living. They would just bank the difference, buy another similar house that needed refurbishment, and repeat the process. Although I didn't realize it at the time, I was getting my first exposure to the world of property, and the dividends it could pay. At that point, my parents certainly couldn't afford to pay for decorators, so the refurbishment team was me, Kamal and our family friends and relatives!

This careful approach helped my parents buy their first corner shop in the early 1970s, which in time led on to a few fish and chip shops and eventually a small portfolio of high street property. Dad's property investing peaked with a deal that was worth around three quarters of a million: not bad for someone who had started with £2 and who had no grounding or advice in the property business whatsoever.

When I wasn't at school, I helped my parents run the shop: stacking the shelves, filling in behind the counter and lugging around massive bags of chapatti flour. Even at that early stage, I was doing a bit of marketing, making little signs to promote prices and products. I'll talk later in the book about how most successful people have had some kind of sales experience at the sharp end early in their career. That was the beginning of mine.

The shop wasn't the only place I was starting to cut my teeth as a salesman. I remember, when I was about nine, Mum taking me to Woolworths on Southall Broadway to buy some football boots. Of course as a kid you want the marque brand, but all we could afford was the £1.99 rip-off version of Adidas. I recall them clearly today, black with red stripes, but there the resemblance to the real deal ended. Even aged nine I knew these weren't made of proper leather. I wore the boots for a season and a half, and then found someone to sell them to for £3. My first proper sale, and a pretty good profit margin too. As my footballing career progressed, I eventually got my hands on some real Adidas boots: real leather this time.

Even in these very early years, some of the traits and habits that would shape my life were being formed. Most obvious is the work ethic that is characteristic of my community, and indeed most immigrant groups. For those who start with nothing, there is no option but to work as hard as you can to try to get a foothold. That has certainly been the experience of most British Asians since my grandfather's generation arrived in the 1950s. I think that's why, even now, I can't really envisage a life in which I don't work, and hope I will still be doing so into my nineties and beyond. The idea of not working feels alien, and I can't imagine myself being satisfied by a life of pursuing only hobbies. Also, in the back of your mind – however far you have travelled from those beginnings, and however much you have made – the need for security and the fear of going back to where it started never really goes away. Hard work remains the best way of ensuring you will never have to.

From my parents, and my grandmother, I inherited traditional Sikh values. Beyond the work ethic, these are about respect and making a contribution to your community. You show respect to others and expect to be respected. And you don't fear anyone, nor do you wish to be feared. Above all, as my mother dinned into us, it is about doing the right thing regardless of whether it is in your self-interest. I have wholly committed to these values throughout my life and career, and they have helped me to create significant goodwill with many people from all walks of life.

Honesty and integrity have lived with me at all times: you can negotiate as hard as you like, but you must never deceive anyone, least of all yourself. And you need to remember that what you sow in life, you will eventually reap. These values were told to us over and over, and reinforced by regular visits to the temple with my devout grandmother, Gurdev Kaur. There I would help scrub the floors, clean the kitchen and serve food to those in need. It reminds you that other people should always come before you. Right up until the end of her life, I took my grandmother to the temple, and I still go on my own at least once a week: a ritual that helps to anchor me and remind me of what's really important. I will forever be indebted to my grandmother and the Sikh values she instilled in me.

It must also be the case that watching my dad's property dealings in some way influenced the direction of my life and career. It was only later, when I started to recognize that the richest and most successful people seemed to have property as a common thread, that I really got interested in it. But throughout my childhood I witnessed, if only in a small way, how money could be made through property. Over the course of my career, I have played in much bigger arenas and with significantly larger pools of capital. But the rules of the game are basically the same regardless of what league you're in, and it was in these early years that I started to learn them.

Racism and rioting

Growing up as an Indian kid in 1960s and 1970s Britain, there was no escaping racism. Southall today is a South Asian community, but that wasn't the case during my childhood. It was still a predominantly white area, despite the growing immigrant population.

My nan, Pritam Kaur, used to tell a story about a time she went to buy a pair of shoes on Southall Broadway. This was in the late 1950s, and she couldn't understand the commotion that surrounded her little shopping expedition, which included someone rushing up to take her photo. It ended up in the *Southall Gazette* as a news story, because she was the shop's first ever Asian customer. This little episode helps to illustrate how far we have come in the decades since, as immigration has created enormous and beneficial changes to the diversity of the UK, and been a great economic and cultural success.

Often the response was more hostile. Because there weren't nearly enough local schools, coaches would arrive every morning to bus the immigrant kids all across London. My school was in Acton, where I was one of few non-white faces. In those years you could have been forgiven for thinking your middle name was Paki. Even after I won a form of acceptance, because I was good at sport and an important player on the football team, the racism didn't really go away. 'You're ok,' people would say to me. 'But the other Pakis aren't.' Football was an important part of my life in these years: it turned out that when you could run faster and kick a ball harder than the others, people started making less fuss about your skin colour. It meant I was in the position of having to look out for the other Asian kids who were being picked on, including my sister.

In my late teens, the racism that had been a persistent feature of our everyday lives started to become a political issue. The National Front (NF) was at its height, stoking fears in the wake of immigration including the rehousing of Ugandan Asians expelled by Idi Amin, a few of whom ended up renting the upstairs room from us in Park Avenue. In 1976, a Sikh schoolboy, Gurdip Singh Chaggar, was murdered in Southall. Three years later, protests against an NF meeting in Southall during the 1979 election campaign sparked race riots, which resulted in the death of an East London teacher.

Two years after that, I was driving home from football training one Friday night through Southall when it became clear something major was starting to happen. The whole of Southall Broadway was at a standstill and police were everywhere, including some in riot gear. Everyone was outside to see what was going on and I soon saw some friends who told me I wasn't going to get the car through and should pull over. As it happened, the next turning was my nan's road, and I parked my burgundy Triumph Dolomite there.

Back on the Broadway, on foot, I found myself in the middle of a full-blown riot. Everything was in chaos: police, skinheads who had flooded into the area to make trouble and Asian kids who had decided to make a stand. For years our parents had kept their heads down and put up quietly with all the racism and abuse. As the second generation came of age, the collective feeling was clear that a line had to be drawn. The anti-NF protests of 1979 had made that clear, and by the spring and summer of 1981 – a time of race riots all across the UK, from Brixton to Toxteth – the resolve had hardened. If a few thousand skinheads had come to make trouble, at least double that number of local Asians came out of their houses to stand against them. Without meaning to, I had become part of the defining moment when British Asians decided to fight back.

All around me things were on fire, from shops and fire engines to the Hambrough Tavern pub, where the disturbance had started around a gig attended by NF members. Suddenly this massive white van, the letters SPG (Special Patrol Group) emblazoned on the side, mounted the pavement right by where I was standing, at speed. I remember throwing myself onto railings on the side of the road to get out of the way. I still earned a baton to the back of the head for my troubles. And I wasn't there to make trouble: I'd just been trying to drive home!

Still clinging to those railings, I looked up to see that it was a Sikh temple, one of the satellite venues for the local community. Of all the places I could have taken refuge, this was the one that presented itself in a time of need – no coincidence in my mind!

After a time, the police started to get the situation under control, and forced the skinheads back up the road towards Hayes. That was going to take them right back past my dad's fish and chip shop. I raced back to my car to get there before the mob could. Having been in the middle of the riot, I knew how serious it was. Dad, who had been listening on the radio, was more relaxed. Despite my attempts to persuade him, he was adamant: his shop, the one he had worked all these years to be able to own, wasn't going to close. I do think that he had enjoyed his evening whisky by this point, which didn't help as far as I was concerned. By this stage, all those around him had shut their shops. Neighbours were coming in to try to plead with him, but he wasn't in the mood to listen. If you want, he said to me, you can go home. He knew what the answer would be: no way would I run away, after all I am a Sikh!

So that is how, as the Southall Riots of 1981 petered out, I stood with my dad and two uncles behind the counter of his shop, four Asian men serving bags of chips to a crowd of NF-tattooed skinheads, with hundreds more packed outside. It was only when a senior policeman pushed his way in and asked Dad to close the shop that he finally complied. An authority figure was able to achieve what family, neighbours and the threat of violence could not. It was a brave thing to do and in such a fractious situation could easily have turned into a foolish one.

That night saw the worst racism I have encountered, but at the same time it was an episode which showed that British Asians were no longer willing to take the abuse lying down. It also showed that when you come from nothing like my father, you will not give it away; while our Sikh roots mean you refuse to be disrespected or give in to racism and violence.

A shirt and tie

Unusually for Asian parents, my mum and dad were never that focused on education. Dad's view especially was that it didn't matter too much if you were educated, as long as you worked hard. So after my school and sixth-form years – which had in any case been more focused on football, and all the things a teenage Sikh boy should not be doing! – I went into my first formal job at the age of eighteen, as a trainee legal executive, having mustered a couple of average A Level grades.

This was unremarkable except for one thing: by doing so I became the first member of my family to do a job that required a shirt and tie. In fact, I don't think I really even knew anyone who had such a job. That was a great symbolic moment, because it meant my life wasn't going to be one of working in factories, foundries and fish and chip shops. Today I rarely wear a suit and tie unless the occasion demands, but to me then it represented everything.

My new job felt important enough that I didn't really mind the fact that, after transport costs from Hayes to Holborn and lunch were taken into account, I wasn't actually making any money from my £139 monthly salary.

On top of the day job, I worked evenings in the chip shop and on the weekends played football to a semi-professional level. But my mates had all gone off to college or university, and I started to feel like I was missing out. Whatever all this was, I knew it wasn't my big picture. With my mother's blessing, and I suspect without my father's, as someone who believed business and hard work was enough, I quit the job and signed up for a course at what was then the Wednesbury Business School. What was supposed to be a temporary return to the Midlands became permanent, and it has been my base ever since. Sandwell in West Bromwich, where I got my business diploma, was also the place that I bought my first house, and where I now fund a school for children marginalized from the mainstream system, including many immigrant children new to the UK: kids who remind me of my own journey.

After graduating in 1983, I took my first job in the business world, with an investment house and mortgage brokerage, Queensway Brokers. For someone with reasonable qualifications by this stage, it had been harder to find employment than it perhaps should have been. I went to plenty of interviews, was punctual, well dressed and I hope eloquent, but the rejections came one after another. I was determined to get a job, as I was having too much fun in Birmingham to leave, and at all costs wanted to avoid going back home to work in the chip shop. But, despite my determination and application, I kept running into dead ends. It's hard to escape the conclusion that there was prejudice involved in this – of the subtle kind, compared to what

I had encountered on the streets of Southall a few years earlier. Racism was changing, and becoming less overt, but it hadn't gone away. I would continue to encounter it for quite some years afterwards.

At Queensway the door finally opened because it was a commission-only job and, frankly, I don't think they cared who was going to take it. But it was an opportunity all the same. When I started, my aim was to earn something in the region of £250 a month. Within twelve months, I was taking home £3,000 a month, and had become the company's top broker.

This was my second experience of formal employment, and both times I ran into problems about pay. In my first job, as soon as I said I wanted to leave, the employer offered to double my salary, the one that had been insufficient to cover my basic expenses. That annoyed me, because if they were willing to increase my pay at this point, they clearly could have afforded to all along. At Queensway, the issue emerged when my results started going through the roof. I discovered that the directors had been holding back some of what should have been my commission earnings.

When the directors then fell out with each other, that was enough for me to throw in my lot with one particular director who was leaving to set up his own business, Bond Wolfe. That became another case of the promised deal not materializing. It quickly became clear he couldn't afford to pay me the salary he had offered, while the BMW that had been dangled as an incentive hadn't turned up either. Confronted, he had to admit that the business was failing and the commissions we should have earned to date had been used to service other debt.

I could have decided to leave, but that would have meant having three different employers on my CV in as many months. Instead,

I tried a different approach. I joined forces with Rory Daly, who had come over with me from Queensway, and who would go on to become my business partner for over three decades. The son of two doctors, Rory was (and is!) an honest and energetic young man of integrity, and a great salesman. We decided to buy the business together. The initial asking price was a laughable £100,000. We ended up paying just 3.5% of that, for a company that has gone on to manage over £5bn in real estate for its clients, employ hundreds of people and spawn a stock market listing for a business with a market cap of over £100m.

We funded the purchase price via a £1,800 overdraft, one that was agreed on a Monday and which by Wednesday we had already exceeded. Today, we probably wouldn't have stood a chance with one of the high street banks. But an 'old school' bank manager, Ian Glaze, believed in us and decided to back us.

With that small line of credit, my life as an entrepreneur was underway at the age of twenty-three. I might have been the first in my family to go to work in a shirt and tie, but now I was following in my father's footsteps as a business owner in my own right. Like many immigrants who struggle to find a job, I would discover that owning your own business is a more accessible route to prosperity.

Lighting the spark

In any business or career there are usually moments that, years later, you look back on as having been pivotal: not just for what you achieved, but what you learned about yourself. One of mine came around the time we bought and relaunched Bond Wolfe. At this stage

I had a business that was just getting off the ground and a house I'd bought in Sandwell Valley that, two years on, was valued at barely more than the purchase price. I knew that if I wanted to get on, I had to make something happen from a standing start. The catalyst for achieving this owed something to my childhood experience of putting up posters around my parents' corner shop.

I had bought my first house in 1984 for £20,500. Two years later, we were starting to see the beginnings of what would become a full-on property boom towards the end of the decade, and I fancied my chances of making a profit. But not according to the local estate agent, Haines and Spires, who said they could get me something in the region of £21,000. Once agent and lawyer fees had been taken off, that was going to mean making a loss. Also, by then I had bought a few more houses for rental at low prices, so I was not looking like a great property investor! But I believed I could create a market and sell homes at a profit.

Undeterred, I decided I would sell the house myself. I wasn't just some guy on the street: we had an office, a business and people who answered the phone. With Rory's support I decided to launch an estate agency business under the Bond Wolfe brand and set an asking price myself for the property of £29,950. The board went up and I sat waiting for the phone to ring. Nothing happened, I waited some more, and still nothing happened.

That left me in an even deeper quandary. The only rational options were to go back to the established estate agent, reduce the asking price, or abandon the sale altogether. Pride wouldn't allow me to do any of those things, and admit defeat on my very first outing into the property market. Instead I resolved to take a different course. All these years later, I'm still not sure what made me do what I did next.

I put up a 'sold' sign!

At this point, the phone did start to ring. People had seen – or thought they had seen – a property selling for almost £10,000 more than the established market value. No one had wanted to buy at that price, but of course they all wanted to sell their houses at that level and they wanted this new estate agent to do it for them. Instructions flowed in and, with the new baseline established, those houses (including a few of mine, for real this time) did sell. In one move, I had proved to myself that I could succeed in property investing, and our business had formally branched out into estate agency. All based on a sale that wasn't really a sale.

Over thirty years later, having done deals that have run into the hundreds of millions, I still look back on that initial sale as my most important. That's partly because it was the first, the one we all need to prove ourselves. More than that, it was something I had created almost out of nothing, where most people would have followed the path of least resistance and taken the property off the market, or lowered the asking price. Refusing to do that, and somehow turning it into a win, was a key moment in my life. It got me going in terms of having a bit of spare capital to play with; and it gave me that inner belief and confidence in my ability to get things done. It got me started, and I haven't stopped in over three decades since.

Riding the waves

That is not to say that the early years were plain sailing. In fact, neither the property management business or estate agency got off to anything like a strong start. Instructions were slow, but we were creative and promised 'no fees' (something we could afford because of the money we made from placing the mortgages). To exacerbate matters, the existing agency establishment in the area was not exactly rolling out the red carpet to this new competitor on its doorstep. Customers had their ears bent not to trust these young pretenders that had only been on the scene two minutes, and who weren't even professional enough to charge fees. Plus we ruffled some feathers ourselves, in the way you do when you're younger and more abrasive. A surveyor once downvalued one of our properties for a bank valuation. When I questioned his credentials and how he had reached that number, he protested to me that he had been doing this for over thirty years and didn't need my help. You can imagine how well he took my retort that, this being the case, it was probably time he learned how to do it properly.

Despite the challenges of establishing ourselves (which came much more from competitors than customers), we were still doing enough for me to put some money aside and over time build up a small portfolio of houses.

I was investing in the right place at the right time, driven by understanding the demand and supply factors as an estate agent. By the late 1980s the property bubble was at its peak and I was able to sell property I'd bought in the region of £10,000–12,000 for prices of up to £40,000, before the recession hit and interest rates went through the roof.

This was the first instance of something that has proved pivotal to my property career: the ability to sense which way the market is moving, and get ahead of it. There have been two major recessions in my career: the early 1990s and the 2007–8 financial crisis. Before both of them, I was close enough to activity on the ground to sense that prices were getting out of control and demand was slackening. This wasn't clairvoyance, but simple market intelligence. As I'll explain later in the book, that is the single most important ingredient of successful property investing.

The advantage of being in the estate agency business is that your ear is close to the ground. When the phone stops ringing all of a sudden, you know before the economic data is published that the market is changing. It's the same running property auctions, which we later branched out into. There's nothing like seeing the empty chairs in an auction room to know that the temperature of the market is changing. That is the time to take winnings off the table and wait out the coming storm. I did that in the late 1980s and again in 2006.

Once the recession has taken hold, and prices have started falling, it's time to go shopping again. In the 1990s I majored in commercial property, which boomed as interest rates came flying down from a peak of over 15%, and rents in some places doubled. Around that boom we built Bond Wolfe into a successful property management and estate agency business, while in parallel developing Bigwood, our property auction company, into the largest of its kind outside of London, with annual sales in excess of £100m. That was all part of the big picture I had set myself in my early twenties, to build a multidisciplinary property business: one where we wouldn't just buy and sell a few bits of property, but do everything related to it – investment, management, auctioning, finance.

In 2007, I looked for the first time to the public markets. I knew that with the possibility of institutional investment, we could accomplish in a matter of years the kind of progress it had taken decades to do privately. With the cash that had been realized from selling commercial property before the downturn, we took a significant stake in Real Estate Investors Plc, the business I now lead as CEO, then a small listed company with a market cap of only a few million. In the teeth of the credit crunch, we went to the city and raised £25m from institutional investors (the first of several successive capital raises during this period which would total over £100m), supported by £10m of our own investment. In the years since, we have grown what was a £20m portfolio into one more than ten times that size, comprising city centre commercial and investment property across Birmingham and the Midlands.

Property investing is a simple business if you do your homework, get the timing right and are prepared to play the long game. I've gone from scrapping over £20,000 properties to owning a multimillion-pound portfolio by applying the straightforward lessons this book will explain. I've prospered by developing an instinct for the property cycle, something that is overlooked by far too many investors. If you can sell when prices are dear and buy when they are cheap, then it's not a very complex business at all.

None of this has been achieved on my own, and I have surrounded myself with an exceptional team of advisers and partners. An outstanding contributor has been Marcus Daly, who is Rory's brother and a qualified accountant. His professionalism, loyalty and commitment have been the heartbeat of our business. He is exceptional at his job and a truly great friend. Marcus and Rory, coupled with my gatekeepers, Anna Durnford, Lisa Worrall and Sue Randell, have been loyal, committed and supportive throughout the journey so far.

Giving back

The religious upbringing I was given has stayed with me throughout my life. I still pray every day, in the morning after waking up, when I enter or leave my home and before I go to sleep. Every week I will make at least one visit to the temple. It's not something I see as a religious belief so much as a set of values and guiding principles for how to live a good life. One of the most important of those is giving back to your community.

To this day, my father returns every January to his village in Bundala, Punjab, to host, at his expense, a sports festival for the children and adults of his village, with thousands of spectators. For my part, over the course of my career I've involved myself in a variety of business and community organizations and charitable ventures: from raising money through charity auctions to sitting on boards and at one stage helping twin Sandwell with Amritsar, home to the holiest pilgrimage site in Sikhism, the Golden Temple. I see it as a responsibility to give back to the community around us in the form not just of money but of time and the use of all the other assets at our disposal. I believe my business has a responsibility to its shareholders, customers, staff and community.

The first thing of this kind I did was to join the board of the Sandwell Chamber of Commerce. I was still in my mid-twenties when I was first approached, a bit disbelieving that what I saw then as a symbol of the establishment would want an Asian kid without much of a track record. It put me in the company of big hitters like Roy Richardson, who with his late brother Don built one of the UK's major property investment and development companies. He and his business were to have a huge impact on me and my career, providing the model of what a highly successful family business in property should look like.

Over time, I came to see the importance not just of organizations like this in their own right, but of representing my community in them. By becoming the first Asian president of the Birmingham Chamber of Commerce, and later the first to become High Sheriff for the West Midlands (a ceremonial role in which you act as the Crown's legal representative and help chaperone royal visits), I was showing that our community could take its place at what had been seen as inaccessible tables. For my children and their peers that is taken as read, but for my parents it would have been unthinkable. For immigrant communities, it's often the second generation that provides the bridge between arrival and integration. That is something I have tried to support wherever possible. Over time, I co-founded what would later become the Institute for Asian Business (now the Asian Business Chamber of Commerce), the largest support group for Asian enterprise in the UK.

Beyond the various charitable and community initiatives, one of the things I'm proudest of is Sandwell Valley School, whose creation in 2014 was funded by the Bond Wolfe charitable trust. This is a school with a particular focus on kids from twelve to eighteen whose needs have not been met elsewhere in the system. Some are refugee or immigrant children whose educational attainment is below what the curriculum demands for their age. Others have experienced bullying or marginalization at school. A number of pupils so far have gone on to college or university. It's not just about them as individuals: I think about the 200 kids in the school now, and the exponential impact they can have in their families and communities by setting a good example and showing what is possible. That could help many hundreds more.

I never expected any formal recognition for this. When my CBE notification letter came through the door it lay unopened for days, because with a government franking I thought it was probably a letter from the Inland Revenue. Awards and recognition aren't really something I focus on: I'm not someone who normally stops to celebrate achievements, preferring to move onto the next deal or priority rather than linger on what is past. But when the day of the ceremony did come – and after the cross-Europe road trip required to get us there – it was hard not to feel something a bit special, especially the experience of going to the Palace with my family.

It was recognition of the journey that had started some sixty-five years ago, with my grandfather getting on the plane to England and changing the course of our family's history. It showed how far we had come from my dad with £2 in his pocket, to him pulling himself up into being a prosperous property owner, and me taking that forward into the businesses I have subsequently built and grown. Even for someone who hates looking back, that was a real moment to stop, reflect and to feel proud. Now, it's on to the next generation of my family to prosper and succeed, something that has become central to my big picture as time has gone on.

What's next?

You'll note that I described that moment as recognition of the journey, and not its culmination. That's because, even at the age of fifty-six, I don't believe I'm even close to the finish line.

One of the reasons is that I still don't see myself as successful, and I'm not being funny or falsely modest when I say that. It's said that '**no man is a success unto himself**' and I probably fit into this category. I've come a long way from when I was doing my first deals in the tens of thousands and the businesses I own and run now are good – but they're still a long way from achieving their potential, and so am I.

There are a few factors at play here. One, which I'll go on to talk more about, is that there's a tendency among successful people not to be satisfied with what you have achieved. You feel like you're doing ok, but it's all about what comes next and not what's happened before. You're only as good as your last deal, even after decades of doing them. The things you've achieved do more to whet your appetite than sate it. You never really lose the motivation that got you started in the first place, in my case the instinctive need for financial security.

Another factor operating is that, running any growing business, you are always expanding the horizons of what is possible. In the case of REI, the company we have now is vastly different from the one we bought into a little over a decade ago. That's not just about the size of the portfolio but also the quality of the management team and the investor base. That means, if we were to keep things going at a steady rate, we'd only be running at a fraction of the capacity the business now contains. The nature of a good business is that its machine is evolving and improving all the time, and that means you have to keep stretching it, like a racehorse, to avoid slackening off. Today I have resources available to me that are considerably greater – from volume of capital to quality of advice and support – than those I had as a young man or even a relatively established entrepreneur. So why would I stop now from continuing to see what can be achieved next? Having evolved from investments and mortgages to estate agency, auctions, property management and property investment, the future for us will be more of the above and diversifying into a finance and bridging business, together with interests in hospitality and private equity.

Finally, there is the generational motivation. At around my stage in life, your focus starts to shift from yourself to how you can support the prospects of your family and people who work with you. My son and nephews have made their way in the property business, independently of me to begin with so that they could learn more than I know and build their own network and knowledge base. And there are people who have now been with me for years, whose careers and potential I also see as my responsibility to keep nurturing. The businesses are now as much about what they will deliver and create for that generation as for me and my partners.

That's an essential motivation for any parent as they reach a certain age. But that doesn't mean I'm done on my own account. There's plenty more I still want to achieve and do, both in business and beyond. As I near my sixtieth birthday, I still think the best lies ahead. I haven't yet achieved the big picture I set myself at the beginning of my career, and it still fires me up as much at the age of fifty-six as it did at twenty-one. I hope and expect the same will be true at eighty-six and ninety-six and beyond. That's the relentlessness in me.

I wanted to make this clear because sometimes books like this are written from the perspective of looking back at a life and career, by people who are focused on the past. Everything I am going to share in the chapters that follow is relevant to the present, mine as well as yours. It's advice I continue to follow and implement in my everyday life and work: the core principles around which I operate and make decisions. I hope it proves as useful to you as it has been – and continues to be – to me.

The future will be rewarding, fulfilling and fun and will take me on a great adventure, but I will never forget my past. I will always remember that I am a Sikh Punjabi grandson of a farmer and son of a factory worker, both of whom have made my journey possible.

2

Understanding success

It's not about being the best. It's about doing your best.

PAUL BASSI CBE

The house I live in today is one I was able to imagine decades before I could eventually afford it. It's almost uncanny. The gates, the driveway, the period architecture – it was all there in my head at the age of twenty-two in January 1984, when I was sat in Birmingham's Midland Hotel with my first proper boss, who was the first person to ask me what I wanted to achieve in my life. When I finally realized the dream years later, it was exactly as I'd visualized: right down to the style of the house and the colour of the drive. As soon as I'd viewed that house, I knew immediately that I was going to buy it, despite the competition.

I believe every successful person has started with a vision like I did, whether it was the business they wanted to build, the house or car they wanted to own, or the life they wanted to achieve for themselves and their family. Sometimes, for a while, the vision looks a little grey or people are afraid to commit to it. But if you keep working at it, the clarity will come, the picture will take shape and your confidence in it will grow. This is necessary, because success doesn't follow vague aspirations or idle hopes. It is achieved by people who have very specific ambitions and ideas about what their future will look like. It's what I like to call the big picture: a guiding mission for your life, and an anchor to keep you on course through all the inevitable ups and downs.

The purpose of this book is to help you work out your big picture and to give you the tools to make it a reality. But before we get to the specific advice about how to do that, and the ways people can achieve success in property, business and beyond, I think it's important to understand exactly what we mean by success. Because this simple and universal concept attracts its fair share of mistaken assumptions and bad advice.

People get a lot wrong about success. They think it's about money, when that's only a measure of success or the means to a more meaningful end. They think it should be judged against the achievements of other people, or someone else's definition of success. And they think that success is only open to certain people, with certain inherent skills.

These are the myths that make people believe success isn't possible for them. They distract people from working out what their big picture in life should be and how they are going to achieve it. They chip away at confidence and self-belief, and mean that some people spend as much time focused on what others are doing as on themselves.

That's why I believe we need a healthier definition of what success is and how it can be achieved. In fact, we should be teaching it in schools as a core academic subject. In a nutshell, I believe that:

- There's nothing difficult, or mysterious, about success.

- Success is determined by desire and attitude, not ability.

- Success is relative: it's about you, not the other guy or girl.

- It's all about the big picture. Don't be afraid to think BIG and learn to dream.

- There are no limits other than the ones you impose on yourself.

- Money is a by-product of success. Strive for success and never chase money.

- You need to work out the why: your motivation to succeed.

There is one thing that unifies all these points: success is about you, and the ability to achieve it is in your hands. It shouldn't be about what someone else wants for you, or what the person over there has done. It should be about your life and the things and people that matter to you. Accepting the power you hold to shape your own life is one of the most important things anyone can do.

Once you've taken ownership of your own future, it's important not to get knocked off course by focusing on the wrong things or worrying too much about other people. You need a balanced and realistic concept of what success looks like if you are ultimately going to achieve it. Here's what my experience tells me that looks like.

There's nothing difficult, or mysterious, about success

'Make real what you make believe.'

JAG SHOKER

In our society we put successful people on a pedestal. Whether that's in business, sport, politics or the arts, our newspapers and screens are dominated by the stories of people who have amassed huge amounts of money, achieved amazing things against the odds, built world-leading businesses and developed game-changing inventions.

To some extent this is a good thing. There's a lot you can learn from studying people who have been successful, and I'm going to talk more about that in the next chapter. It's exactly what I did at the beginning of my career. One of the reasons I got into the property business in the first place was that, having looked at the people topping all the rich lists in the 1980s, it was obvious that real estate was something most had in common. I became a property investor because that looked like what successful people did and how they made their money. A simple lesson that set up the whole of the rest of my life, one that began with observing my parents and over time grew by learning from outstanding family businesses in property including Caledonia Investments and Richardson Capital.

But while we should study successful people and companies, it's easy to be put off by the way success is generally portrayed in society and through the media today. The issue with our tendency to fetishize success and successful people is that it can be discouraging and demotivating. If you're sitting at home reading that success means private islands, racehorses and Beyoncé singing at your birthday party, it's all going to seem too distant to even bother with. What relevance does that have if you're thinking about how to buy your first house or car? It feeds the belief that success is something only other people can achieve: that it's difficult and mysterious, a secret destination to which only the lucky few are granted directions.

This couldn't be further from the truth. There is no big secret to success, only good habits, the ability to make the most of opportunities, and what you learn from experience. Throughout this book I will talk about the traits that successful people have in common, behaviours you can seek to mimic and tactics you can use. But none of that is worth anything unless you accept that success is at its core a straightforward thing. It's about making the most of the circumstances around you, and using the tools at your disposal to meet short-term goals and move towards your big picture. The playing field is a lot more level than most people think. But to take advantage of that, first you have to believe it. And that comes by acknowledging that the secrets to success aren't really that secret after all. Remember the saying, **'What the mind can conceive and believe, the mind can achieve.'**

Success is determined by desire and attitude, not ability

In the same way that some people believe success is difficult and mysterious, they think successful people have been blessed with special abilities. This might be true for elite athletes, or perhaps some artists. But it couldn't be more wrong when it comes to business and property.

Take my own career. There isn't a single deal I've done that wasn't available to anyone else in the property world. Pretty much every time, the difference was my willingness to pick up the phone and pursue an opportunity that I'd seen based on public information. That's got much more to do with desire and attitude – being relentless in your work – than it does skill or ability.

Almost always, the difference between one person succeeding and another not doing so comes down to who is willing to put the work in: to chase up leads, to go out and cultivate a network that means you will know the right person at the right time, and to really do your research properly. Anyone can do those things: it doesn't matter what school you went to or what your exam results were. It's not about being clever or having particular talents: it's about your desire to go out and make things happen; and your attitude to obstacles and challenges. This is the relentlessness that really makes the difference, because you can't just do a bit of these things occasionally. You have to do a lot of them, all of the time, to be successful. And there is nothing stopping you from doing just that. So don't let anyone work harder than you do.

It's true that some people have advantages in life, whether that is the inheritance of wealth, a contacts book or indeed an entire business. But the most important attributes when it comes to success are also the most democratic: the ability to be the hardest worker, the most diligent networker, the most proactive opportunity-seeker and the most persuasive negotiator. Those are skills and behaviours that anyone can develop. There is no success gene, or at least nothing that's remotely as powerful as the things I've just described.

So, the next time you are looking at someone successful and wondering how they've done it, don't assume that they rose easily to the top on the basis of natural talent. Instead, consider the hard work it probably took to get there: the amount of time, effort and desire it demanded to become the supreme expert or practitioner in their field. Successful people can seem effortless, but that is rarely the reality of how they made it. Most are like the swan, looking outwardly serene but paddling furiously beneath the surface. That's a good thing, because if they had to work hard to get there, and rely on their attitude and desire rather than inherent ability, then the same opportunity is open to the rest of us.

Success is relative: it's about you, not the other guy or girl

My dad arrived in this country in the late 1950s with just £2 to his name. I built a business that has managed over £5bn worth of property for clients and employed hundreds of people. But I think the truth is that he was more successful than I've been.

And that's because success is relative, not absolute. It's not about material gains, but the extent to which you fulfil your potential in life, given your own specific circumstances.

For my dad, as a first-generation immigrant, starting with absolutely nothing and having to work poorly paid factory jobs to get by, the crowning achievement of buying up a parade of high-street shops, and living in the stockbroker belt of Gerrards Cross in Buckinghamshire, was extraordinary. From his starting point, he travelled further and climbed higher than I have, from a non-English-speaking immigrant to a millionaire in twenty-five years.

It's important to understand that success is relative in the same way that you need to accept that there is nothing mysterious or difficult about it. For one person, success might mean earning £400 a week, while for another it will feel like a failure if they don't make £1m every month. The threshold of what delivers security and contentment is going to vary a lot depending on your circumstances.

Only by accepting that success is relative can you focus on your own needs and not get distracted by those around you. It's all too easy to spend your whole life watching other people, tracking their achievements and wondering how well they are doing. The problem then is that you start to buy into the corrosive idea that success is something that happens to other people and which you can't have for yourself.

That's why I will often use the phrase, **'Don't be the man who talks about the man; be the man the man talks about.'** It's about putting the onus on yourself to succeed and focusing on what you can be doing, rather than worrying about everyone else. To be successful you need to focus on your own big picture and the goals that will move you towards it. Everything to do with other people in your life or industry is ultimately a form of distraction or displacement activity. You're never going to make progress while you're admiring someone else's achievements or worrying that they're doing better than you are. Instead, you have to forget about the unhelpful game of compare and contrast, and look to yourself.

In the end, it really doesn't matter if the other guy has just bought a yacht or another holiday home. Let them worry about that, because it has no bearing whatsoever on your big picture. Success is relative, and it's about achieving fulfilment in your own life, on your own terms. It's got nothing to do with other people unless you let it.

It's all about the big picture. Don't be afraid to think BIG

I was lucky that the very first time anyone asked me what I wanted to achieve with my life, I instinctively knew the answers. It was the house that I was eventually able to buy, decades later – one with gates, a driveway and gardens, a world away from the cramped Southall terrace that I'd grown up in – and it was a multidisciplined, highly successful, city-centre property business.

Often people will talk about goals in life and business, but I draw a distinction between these and a big picture. Goals are what you need to set and achieve the whole time. You will start every week, every quarter and every calendar year with goals to hit. Goals are incremental and constantly evolving, whereas the big picture, once it has settled in your mind, never really changes. It's the consistent, long-term ambition that sums up what you want to achieve in your life: the end-point and not all the staging posts along the way. Simply put, it is your ultimate destination. As someone once said, '**Go big or go home.**'

You need a big picture to sit above all your short- and medium-term goals, so that you never lose sight of what all the work you're doing is about. Whatever your career, sometimes you are going to question why you're working so hard and what the point really is. It's in those moments of doubt and despondency that the big picture will pull you through. It helps you to remember that there's something more at stake here than the next deal you are hunting down. That work is serving a higher purpose: moving you closer to your big picture and the life you have always dreamed of living and providing for your family.

Some of you, like me thirty-five years ago, might already know exactly what that big picture looks like. Others will have a hazy idea that needs clarifying, and others might say that they don't know where to start (though I think the truth is that everyone does have a vision of some sort, if they are prepared to be honest with themselves). Whatever the case, there are two things that your big picture needs to be:

1. It needs to be BIG and motivational for you!

There's no point in setting a big picture that you could achieve in the next week, or even the next few years. This needs to be something life-defining, that will leave you feeling fulfilled once it has been achieved, not wondering if you set the bar too low. I didn't just have a dream of being able to afford my own house; I had a big picture which was the kind of property I knew it would take me decades to build towards – something that seemed a million miles away to me as a twenty-two-year-old, but which I knew other people had, and which I could too if I worked hard enough.

I took the same attitude when setting up my first property business, also in my early twenties. I didn't want to be another amateur who made a bit of money here and there from buying, doing up and then selling on residential properties. I wanted a big, multidisciplined property business: one that could put me in the same arena as all those rich-listers I'd clocked who were making their money from property investment. I realized that what my dad had been doing was just scratching the surface. In addition to buying and selling, I could also own property, manage it for other people and branch out into commercial investments, auctions and finance. I wanted all of that and the opportunities it held, not just the small slice of the market that I already knew.

That is a fundamental lesson for anyone, whether you are working out your big picture or thinking about the career or business you will build to get there. You need to think big, stretching beyond what you know and are familiar with, to fulfil your ambitions in life.

2. It needs to be yours

As someone who has employed and mentored hundreds of people over the years, one thing I've often thought is that people get institutionalized in their goal-setting. There's such a powerful narrative peddled that you need to get your GCSEs and A Levels and work your way into a profession and a steady career. It can be hard for people to separate what they want for themselves from what their family, or indeed society, wants for them.

It's certainly true that the 'traditional' life path is not as clear cut as it once seemed. More young people are becoming entrepreneurs and making their own way. There is a lot more flexibility in how and where people can work. Technology has changed the landscape but it remains the case that too many people outsource their ambitions and let others set the terms of what they want in life.

My advice to the people I mentor is always to set aside what they think the 'right' answers are and to try to forget what their parents or others are telling them to do. Family and friends might have your best interests at heart, but only you know what really motivates you and what your own big picture looks like, one that will drive you to work relentlessly over years and decades to achieve. So don't let anyone, however well intentioned, direct your destiny. Make sure your big picture is personal, rooted in the things that matter most to you and something that you know in your heart you will keep on fighting to achieve, whatever obstacles come in your way.

There are no limits other than the ones you impose on yourself

People are often their own worst enemy in life. We blame bad luck and other people for things going wrong, when the true cause is often closer to home. If I was to identify the most common reason that people fail to succeed, it would be the limitations they place upon themselves: what I call 'limiting beliefs'.

In the end, the basic truth is that you are only as good as you believe yourself to be. If you can't see yourself rising beyond your current position at work, earning more than you currently earn or living in a nicer house than you currently do, then I can guarantee none of those things will ever happen.

Limiting beliefs are the barrier to success in many lives. People who don't think they can do a certain thing, or achieve a certain goal, are never going to. There's zero chance of mustering the necessary self-belief if your starting point is one where you don't have faith in yourself. You can't be relentless about something in which you have no essential confidence.

That doesn't mean you should be mindlessly confident about things. If you haven't put on a pair of trainers in years, don't go out and try a marathon first time. Whatever some may say, it isn't true that self-belief can overcome every barrier.

But you do need to understand the psychology of the limiting belief and the role it plays in your life. That starts with recognizing where these beliefs come from, which is us. We are the ones who tell ourselves about what we can and can't do, what we are and aren't good at and what we should and shouldn't be attempting. There generally aren't loads of people who are standing in our way or trying to trip us up. It might seem that way, but often the barriers have been dreamt up in our own heads, and the inhibition is all to do with us.

Just as we endlessly compare ourselves to other people, we also worry about what they think about us and what their motivations are. But the real truth is as the American author Olin Miller once wrote, **'You'll worry less about what people think of you when you realize how seldom they do.'**

If you want to achieve more than you think you're capable of, the first step is to accept that those limitations aren't real. There is no great independent adjudicator saying you are allowed to do this or that, and only these people are allowed to achieve such and such a thing. Only you can give yourself permission to have a go at something, and only you can stop yourself from trying.

Accepting personal ownership over this, and taking responsibility for your actions rather than pretending some hidden force is holding you back, is a hugely liberating thing. It simplifies a question that lots of people make complicated, which is how can I make progress and what do I do next? It allows you to start breaking through what you once perceived as your limits, because you've recognized that they weren't real after all. Once you've realized that limiting beliefs are a bit of a psychological con that we play on ourselves, nothing is going to stop you from moving forwards.

Money is a by-product of success. Strive for success and never chase money

'Enough is enough, more will end in tragedy.'

PAUL BASSI CBE

'Who here wants to earn a million?' That was the question I once posed to a room of about 500 bankers. As you will imagine, almost every hand went up. My response? 'That's bollocks.'

People laughed, because the last thing bankers expect to hear is that there's anything wrong with making money. And you might be equally surprised when you read this next bit. You might not believe me when I say that no one really wants to make money. But it's true. They don't. And anyone who comes into my office and says that their goal in life is to be a multimillionaire is lying to themselves. That's not what they want.

Allow me to explain. Of course money is important, but we need to understand what it's actually for. It's the means to achieve the things we want in life. And it's one of the best ways of measuring how well we have done. But that's all it is: an enabler and a measure, a way of keeping score.

Money can make your big picture happen, but it can never *be* the big picture. And if someone says it is, they're either lying or haven't worked out what they really want, and almost certainly won't achieve it.

Whenever anyone tells me that money is their life's ambition, I tell them to go away and think harder. Because I know that's not what anyone really wants from their life. It's what the money buys that they want: the cars, yachts and houses, the things you can do for your friends and loved ones, a community cause you can support, even for some the status and reputation it can help you to achieve, the opportunity to make a point, prove somebody wrong or make someone proud.

That's why it's a mistake to put money on a pedestal. Of course, you can and should enjoy making money. It shows you are succeeding and moving towards your big picture. But you should also be clear-sighted about what making money is really about: achieving the truly important, meaningful things. It's about being able to have what you want and not worry about you or your family ever wanting for anything. But it's never, never about money for its own sake.

The Apple founder Steve Jobs captured this brilliantly, in words that have been attributed to him on his deathbed: '**I realize that all the accolades and riches of which I was once so proud, are now insignificant to me. I have little joy in my life and wealth is only a fact of life that I am accustomed to. Only now I understand that once you accumulate enough money for the rest of your life, you must pursue objectives that are not related to wealth.**'

No one sits on their deathbed counting their money. As I found out after suffering a serious heart problem in my late forties, the prospect of death is something that clarifies what really matters in life. And that definitely isn't money.

My point is not just that money shouldn't be your goal, but that it categorically isn't. I can promise you, if you think your big picture in life is about the bank balance, then you haven't got there yet. You don't yet know what it is you really want to achieve.

But once you do work that out, in many ways it accelerates your need and desire to make money. Because now you are doing it for a purpose;

your efforts are not just about money in isolation, but the things you know to be important and which money will help you to achieve.

True enrichment in life is not about making money, and money alone has never delivered fulfilment to anyone. So as you set out towards achieving your big picture, it's essential that you recognize what money is and what it's for. It's the enabler, not the end goal. And that's why it's true that no one really *wants* to make money, however much they might need to.

You need to work out the why: your motivation to succeed

To understand what your big picture really is, you need to tap into the things that really motivate you. In all of us, there is something that drives us to get up and go each morning: something that explains who we are and the choices we make in life.

Sometimes that motivation is positive: a desire to help others or to make a difference. And it can be grounded in a negative: wanting to prove someone wrong or to beat the competition. I recall my history teacher, Mrs Perry, saying 'Bassi, you will never amount to anything!' In doing so, she actually helped me more than she could ever have realized.

Whatever their source, these motivations are our deepest hopes and fears in life: often those that are a legacy of childhood experience and upbringing. Once all the pretence has been stripped away, they are who we really are as people.

The important thing is that you recognize what really motivates you, and are honest with yourself about it. You need to understand

and acknowledge the 'why' in your life if your big picture is going to become clear and achievable.

The 'why' in my life is and always has been security. When you've come from an immigrant family who started with next to nothing, security is something you crave. You never want to have to go back to the financial starting point of your parents or grandparents. So much work has gone into getting to this point, and you will do anything to avoid backsliding and ending up back where you began, disrespecting all that hard work that your parents and grandparents did.

Everything I have done in my life has been driven by the need for security and to create stable foundations. My big picture was the dream home and the property business, both of which are ultimately manifestations of the desire for stability: the biggest possible contrast to the houses where my parents lived in the 1960s and 1970s and the jobs they had to work to make ends meet.

Everyone's big picture is rooted in something, and each one of us needs to understand what that is. This intrinsic motivation is often deeply personal and not something you are likely to shout about in public. But in your own mind, it needs to be clear, and you need to be honest with yourself. Understanding what you want to do is one essential foundation of being successful; but understanding why you want to do it is just as important. Your big picture will never be complete or achievable until you take the time to understand and accept what is producing it.

My intention in this chapter has been to give you an insight into how to think about success: to see it as something achievable rather than intimidating, and to set aside some of the myths that surround it:

from the need to have 'talent' to the idea that we are motivated by money.

I want you to be clear-sighted about the things that trip many people up: from 'limiting beliefs' that exist only in our own heads, to focusing more on other people than you do yourself.

The most important thing to remember is that there is no one and nothing stopping you from pursuing your big picture. That's not to pretend it will be easy. Once you start trying to build a business or climb the career ladder, there are going to be plenty of people in your way. But none of them are stopping you from making a start and having a go.

Often, the hardest opponent you will face is yourself: the limits you place on your own abilities and ambitions, and the emphasis you give to the achievements of others. If there is a first step to being successful in life, it is ridding your mind of all the wrong ideas that suggest success is difficult or 'not for me'.

That, as I told the room of 500 bankers, is bollocks. Anyone can be successful, but only if they first believe that to be possible. So, before we go further and start to get into the nitty gritty, ask yourself a simple question. Do you believe it is possible?

3

Understanding successful people

The superior man is modest in his speech, but exceeds in his actions.
CONFUCIUS

If you want to understand how to do anything in life, look around you. There are few things that someone else hasn't already tried, tested and perfected a method for. Everything they discovered, did wrong, learned and changed along the way is a valuable experience and insight that you can use. Why wouldn't you take advantage of that?

Learning how to be successful in life is really no different from learning how to drive a car. Because it can be learned: there are things you have to know how to do, and others you need to learn not to. There is a right way to do things and there are dangerous alternatives: good habits that set you on the right path, and mistakes that will send you careering off the road.

I found my highway code for being successful by studying other successful people and reading extensively. Over the course of my career, as I have come to work with and know well a whole range of highly accomplished entrepreneurs and businesspeople, it has become clear quite how much they have in common. There are shared traits that provide a roadmap for anyone who wants to be successful.

Technique is important, and we will cover that regarding business and property in the chapters that follow. But the first and most important thing is to have the right outlook and approach to life, both personal and professional. It's about how you think, behave, treat others and approach the challenges and opportunities of your life. And it's about things that are embedded deep in you, from childhood experience onwards.

These are observations and not advice points. Some relate to life circumstances that are outside our choice and control. You might not relate to all of them, but it helps to recognize them and to map them against your own life experience: appreciating both what it takes to be successful and what elements of your own history you can harness to good effect. Before you start to plot your own journey to success, you need to understand how other successful people have done it, and the many disciplines and characteristics it has required of them.

Given my career, and the people I have moved with, inevitably the focus is on business and property, but I believe the points in this chapter apply to success in any walk of life. The skills may be very different, but ultimately successful entrepreneurs have much more in common with great athletes, musicians, teachers and politicians than they do differences. The fundamental traits are very much the same.

Based on thirty-five years of my own career and the many outstanding people I have observed along the way, here is what makes successful people tick.

They are positive, and see all obstacles as opportunities

Positivity is a word that can easily be misunderstood. There is a genre of self-help advice that says you can smile and laugh your way past all of life's problems, and that the power of optimism and positivity alone can carry you through. That's not what I'm talking about here. What I mean by positivity is the attitude you take to your life and career, and the outlook you have on the various things that will come your way, both good and bad.

This is especially important at moments of change, when fortunes are there to be made. If I was to summarize why I have done well as a property investor, it would be that I have taken advantage of fluctuations in the market, riding the property cycle so that my entry price is always as low as possible, and the price of sale much higher. When I've sensed a recession coming, I've taken my winnings off the table ahead of time. And when a recession does hit, I get back into the market to buy when others are running scared. As Warren Buffett famously said, as an investor you need to be fearful when others are greedy, and greedy when others are fearful.

There are all sorts of things you need to underpin those decisions: market intelligence, experience about how cycles work and an understanding of how to do deals and manage properties. But none of that would count for anything without a positive approach. Because it doesn't matter how expert a surveyor, dealmaker and manager you are; if you look at a building on the market and see only its problems, where I see an opportunity in the making, only one of us is going to end up making any money.

No one becomes successful without making some moves and taking some risks. Being positive allows you to see opportunities where others are too busy weighing up the downsides to do anything.

Positivity is also about vision and being able to see the big picture. If you talk to an entrepreneur just starting out, who might still be working out of their kitchen or a tiny office, they won't tell you about the business they have now: its shortcomings, problems and the challenges it faces to survive. They're going to tell you about the business they want to build: all the people they are going to hire, the products they are going to build and the impact they are going to make on the world. That is positivity – the ability to see ahead and map your way towards a big picture, in a way that brings other people with you.

It's the same in property. When I buy a building, it's with a clear idea of the changes we are going to make to it, how it will improve and the value it will accrue before an eventual sale. Positivity means you look to the long-term opportunities and don't allow immediate hurdles to get in the way of realizing them.

That is why successful people often do some of their best work when the majority are worried and ducking for cover. Where many see obstacles, the successful see opportunities. It's not that they don't see the obstacles – they just don't take them particularly seriously, and they certainly won't fight shy of them. The most entrepreneurial and successful people welcome these hurdles, because they know a lot of their competitors are going to trip up. The herd is going to thin, the competition is going to slacken and the field is going to open up to those who have stayed the course, which means you. In our case, we were happy in the early 1990s when interest rates were 15% and everybody withdrew from property, and when most investors were running for cover after the 2008 financial crisis, we raised capital and spent £200m on property whose value has appreciated significantly in the years since.

They are self-driven and instinctive, with a relentless work ethic

I discussed in the last chapter how a big picture is fundamental to success, and it follows that you won't meet a successful person who doesn't have one. Because of the immense hard work required to be genuinely successful in any field, you need the motivation and drive of a big picture to keep going. There needs to be something bigger than the problems you are dealing with in a given day, week or month.

The big picture provides the mainstay of your motivation. But there is usually something more driving on successful people. They are often trying to prove something to someone, and to earn recognition from those who matter to them. That's particularly true for those of us who came from poor or marginalized backgrounds, which also helps explain why immigrant communities are generally the source of significant upward mobility and economic success.

I think back to a time early in my career when I rang up the West Bromwich Building Society, seeking a loan to purchase some buy-to-let properties. They didn't just turn down the application; they weren't even interesting in talking to me. The response was about as dismissive as you could get. That was in the late 1980s. About thirty years later, the West Bromwich Building Society was struggling and needed to sell its head office. I knew their agents well. In fact, I had their 1980s phone number memorized (0121 236-8236) because I used to ring them up so often in the early days, and they too couldn't get me off the phone quick enough. Now, of course, they wanted my business. I am a known buyer in the market, there was a crisis unfolding and they needed to sell. Would I like to buy this office? I did, and made a seven-figure profit selling it on. A good deal, but an especially sweet one given the history. Stack up those rejections early on in your journey: they often provide some of the most powerful motives to succeed.

It doesn't matter what background you come from, in all our lives there are setbacks and rejections. Successful people make good use of these and set out to prove the naysayers wrong, just like I did my history teacher at school. You need that drive to be successful: not just a big picture you are motivated to realize, but the desire to disprove the thing someone once said about you or did to you. Motivation is a fundamental part of how we get on in life. The most successful people are the ones who find the strongest and most enduring motivation from their life experiences, and then squeeze out every last drop of it to keep going and going, towards and beyond their goals.

They are also people who are accustomed to the real meaning of hard work. This is the question that tends to separate the 'sort of successful' from the very successful. If someone's definition of hard work is that they do everything that is asked of them, work as long as they need to and never miss a deadline, then that takes you so far. But it's not enough.

The most successful people are the ones who recognize that there is no such thing as 'enough', or 'done'. You're never finished building a business or fleshing out a big picture. There will always be more you could be doing – to improve your market intelligence, build your network and seek out opportunities. Moderately successful people have a point where they want to stop, go home and take a break. The most successful are relentless, and often don't know when to stop. They're never done or satisfied. It's always about what comes next. I had never thought about it in those terms until my colleague Andrew Osborne, an ex-Goldman Sachs property investor, used the word relentless to describe our business. And then it hit me: I am, our business culture is, and so are all of the successful people I have encountered over the years.

They get principles, not detail; and focus on solutions, not problems

Everyone who is successful in business knows the ins and outs of their company, the industry they operate in, and their competition. But that doesn't mean they are apprised of everything that's going on, all of the time. They will be perfectly capable of getting stuck into the detail of a deal or particular problem, but most of the time they will choose not to.

That is because of their unerring focus on the big picture: where all of this work is ultimately taking them and the people around them. Detail matters immensely, but successful people don't get caught up in it to the exclusion of their big picture. As the captain of the ship you can't be responsible for fighting every battle every day, but you can be the one who makes sure the boat is still pointing in the right direction. What's more, there's no way of navigating your way towards a big picture if your focus is on what's happening below deck. And along the way, you may have to **'lose a few battles to win the war'.**

Think about the term micromanager. You've never heard that used in a positive sense about anyone. It describes a person who gets involved in too many details that shouldn't concern them, impedes their team and ultimately takes their eye off the ball. Successful people don't micromanage. They surround themselves with brilliant people who ensure that all the important details are being looked after. They keep their focus on the big picture, only diving into the weeds when it's necessary or helpful to help resolve a problem.

Even for someone with the kind of relentless work ethic I have just described, there is only so much time, attention and focus to go around. Successful people will work as hard as anyone, but they are also efficient in how they go about it, focusing their efforts on the most important things. They work smart, recruit smarter people and always keep their eyes fixed on the thing that matters above all: the big picture.

For the same reason, successful people don't like to dwell on problems and tend to get impatient with those who table an issue without an idea of how they are going to resolve it. The fact is that 99% of business problems can be easily understood and diagnosed. In my industry it usually comes down to something as straightforward as tenants being unhappy, a problem with the building, or the level of income from a property falling. The problem is not hard to identify: it takes one or two sentences to convey it, not a five-hour seminar. The only real question is what you are going to do about it.

Again, this is often a relatively straightforward business of making a change: dropping the rent if a tenant is threatening to leave or agreeing to let them go because you know you can replace them at a similar or higher rent; changing the agent if they haven't got the job done; refurbishing the building if it's in need of some TLC. Some people in business obsess about problems and almost wallow in them, talking endlessly about what is going wrong and why. Successful entrepreneurs and executives take the opposite approach. They go straight to the solution, the thing they can do, and the change that will most likely make a difference. They are relentless in their focus, filtering out the peripheral and applying themselves only to the genuinely important issues.

They think differently, and their view is sometimes distorted

Back in the 1980s, an employee at Apple said that company founder Steve Jobs had a 'reality distortion field'. It's something you will often hear said about entrepreneurs: that they don't see things the same way as the people around them, and have ideas that can seem out of tune or even unrealistic.

Entrepreneurs can frustrate the people they work with because they often don't go for the obvious solution that everyone is trying to push on them. Even when the answer seems to be staring them in the face, they sometimes have a different view and an alternative plan.

That ability to, in the words of the famous Apple advertising campaign, 'think different' is the essence of entrepreneurship. It means you are coming at things from a different angle, getting away from the herd and developing ideas that will distinguish your company from the competition.

The most dangerous thing to do in business is to copy everyone else. As James Goldsmith, the billionaire investor, once said, **'If you see a bandwagon coming, it's too late.'** If you are surrounded by others with the same ideas as you, trying to pursue the same opportunities through the same channels, there is limited space and many will miss out. By contrast, the nirvana is to be in completely unoccupied territory: where it's your product or no product, your price or none at all. Of course, the latter is a rare if not impossible state to achieve, but a core trait of successful people is that they know how to get themselves away from the herd and into a relative greenfield.

And it's not just in business. The most successful people in all fields are often those who approach the problem in a different way. And often they get criticized for trying something new or outside the mainstream. American athlete Dick Fosbury was branded the 'laziest high jumper in the world' in the late 1960s when he broke with convention and started jumping backwards over the high bar rather than using the traditional scissor kick. Now you won't find a high jumper from school level to the Olympics who doesn't follow his once-mocked method.

Humanity only progresses and changes because there are people who don't see the world the way most people do, and who uncover opportunities to do things differently or better. It's precisely this ability that has allowed us to create the advanced, technological society we live in today. It's what is described in Japan as 'Kaizen', the process of continuous improvement, seen as the key to fulfilling lives and sustainable businesses.

Thinking differently doesn't have to be about changing the world. It can be as simple as looking at the market you work in through a different lens. In my own career, it meant going against the advice of surveyors and agents who had a very clear concept of what a good investment looked like.

The consensus view was that a company like mine should be looking at prime city-centre commercial property. This, everyone kept telling me, was the safe and sensible option. But I saw it differently. To me, at a stage in my career when I wasn't flush with capital, commercial real estate looked expensive. And it felt risky too, given that in most cases you are exposed to a single corporate tenant. Instead we focused on office blocks in the Black Country, where the buildings were a quarter of the price and you had ten tenants instead of one. These offices weren't prestige purchases, but they offered exactly what I was looking for: an affordable entry price, good rental income and the scope for capital appreciation and diversity of occupier. If one tenant went bust or decided to leave, I still had another nine to rely upon. To others these seemed like distressed assets with little worth, but they were a large part of our success in the early years, because we looked past the unpromising exterior and saw the fundamental value.

That experience taught me an essential lesson: you want to be where the market opportunity is, but the mainstream market isn't. In the 1990s, I had done the same by shifting from buying residential to high-street property, shrinking the competitor pool from thousands of others to just a handful.

What some see as a distorted view, others regard as an obvious opportunity or alternative that hasn't yet been considered. Successful people don't operate within the parameters of their trade: they find ways to extend, expand and change it. That is the power and importance of being able to think differently.

They're ultimately salespeople, who will have undertaken sales at the sharp end

Whatever your career, it is almost certain that you are selling something, whether that is a product, your time or ideas, or yourself. We sell ourselves to earn, to get noticed and to get ahead. And we sell to survive. You can't get funding for your business, the support of shareholders, or people to work for you, unless you have the ability to sell. This goes well beyond business. We are selling ourselves throughout our lives: to be selected ahead of others to get a job, win a promotion or find a life or business partner.

But there is selling and then there is selling. And what I've noticed about the most successful people I know is that they aren't just natural salespeople, but have usually done something early in their life or career that saw them having to sell at the sharp end. And I really mean the sharp end: cold calling (which I did when starting out as a mortgage broker) and door knocking.

There's nothing quite like having a door slammed in your face, or a phone hung up on you, to start understanding the tough realities of how to do business and win customers. Selling makes you resilient, because it is a high-volume, low-output job, where frequent failure is inevitable. It encourages you to be proactive, because you often need an unconventional approach to get through people's indifference or hostility. And it means you are in the mind of your customer, working out what motivates them, which is the only way you can succeed in any kind of business.

That may help explain why some of the most successful business leaders of our time, from Warren Buffett to long-time Starbucks CEO

Howard Schultz, began their career in sales jobs. Early sales experience – whether in a formal first job, or even through childhood experience like the years I spent working in my parents' corner shop – prepares you in many important ways for the tough realities of building a business or successful career. Scratch the surface of most successful people – entrepreneurs, politicians, lawyers – and you will find a salesperson underneath: someone who knows instinctively how to advocate for themselves and their product, and who is an experienced persuader of people. Whatever the differences in their personality and profession, most of the truly successful people you will meet are sellers at their core.

They are likely to have excelled at sports

Alongside the sales experience will often come some form of excellence in sport. Fortune estimates that 95% of the CEOs of Fortune 500 companies played sport when they were younger. It's not a boys' club thing either. A survey by the accountants EY found that 96% of women with C-suite positions had played sport at school or university, while two-thirds had continued to do so during their careers.

Sport offers some of the same fundamental training for life success as sales. The competitive aspect teaches you to stand up for yourself, to rely on your skills and mentality, and to work with and lead others around you.

People who excelled at sport also have one of the essential ingredients to succeed in any field, which is confidence. It is confidence

– which isn't inherent, but evolves over time and derives from your life experiences – that equips you to make important decisions and take risks. Confidence turns you from someone who hesitates over opportunities to a person who pursues them with full force.

But remember, that kind of confidence doesn't just come from winning. Every sporting career, even at the most junior level, involves its share of ups and downs. We've all won and lost, been picked and dropped, and felt the pain of defeat or rejection as much as the elation of victory. These are all experiences that help shape you as a person, and take away the notion that you are in any way untouchable. You're that much better prepared for the knocks you will encounter in life and work if you have learned to deal with them at an early age, in a setting where there is always an opportunity to try again and succeed next time. You learn that injuries and losses are as much a part of the game as goals and titles.

I mentioned in the last chapter that football was an important part of my early life. It was by excelling at football that I was able to win a degree of acceptance amid the racism that was the norm in my 1970s schooldays. But football did more than just help me survive the rough and tumble. It was also character-building in several important ways. I remember very clearly the first competitive match I played for my school (also, for reasons that will become obvious, the last game my dad ever came to watch me in). At that point I had a pretty high opinion of myself, based on playground games. But this was a different story. We got hammered 10–0, a crushing experience but ultimately a defining one. It taught me that, however good you think you are, there is always a next level, a fiercer arena, and one that demands that you learn and improve in order to compete.

That isn't just a sporting reality: it's a life lesson that applies at every stage and in every area. Very few people can be said to have reached the undisputed peak of their profession. For the rest of us, there is always another level of excellence to aspire to, always another competitor above us, and that means the process of self-improvement can never, and should never, end. Sport teaches you that, and it's a lesson that the most successful people never forget and never stop implementing.

They're likely to have been promiscuous in their twenties and thirties

It's no great secret that success and sex drive often go hand in hand. Studies have found clear correlations between higher earnings and people who have sex more often. This is far from a novel observation. The early twentieth-century management author Napoleon Hill wrote a chapter in his book, *Think and Grow Rich,* which has sold over 15 million copies, about how high sex drive was a common feature among the successful people he had interviewed in his study.

It's not difficult to understand why this is the case. Many of the attributes we need to attract sexual partners are the same needed to be successful in life. You have to be charming, to show confidence in yourself that transmits itself to others, and you need desire. And you have to be able to sell yourself. Because what is a first date really, except a relationship interview by another name?

As I've said, successful people are often those who obtain early experience in sales. And one of the ways many put that sales flair to the test is in finding sexual partners in their twenties and thirties. It might not sound romantic but it's still true: we have to sell ourselves to those around us, and the people who were good at selling themselves in their twenties in a nightclub (or today on a dating app) will often become those who are good at selling themselves for a job, and at selling deals that run into the tens or hundreds of millions. The instinct to sell and achieve is embedded from an early age and it finds different outlets at all the different stages in life.

Sexual promiscuity is not necessarily the most attractive trait of successful people, but it's undoubtedly a common factor. It's tied in with many of the impulses and behaviours that drive people to be successful in the first place: competitiveness, self-confidence and the desire to be accepted by others. If it wasn't true, there wouldn't be so many sex scandals among high-ranking politicians, for example. Why else would you risk reputational ruin unless it was a fundamental part of your make-up to seek out exactly that danger? Whether we, or they, like it or not, the pursuit of sex and the pursuit of success are often inextricably linked.

They will have been let down by a parent or have a point to prove to family, friends or critics

It would be a mistake to assume that successful people have led privileged lives, floating through one open door after another. In fact, the opposite is often true. Many of the biggest success stories are of people who have either come from nothing or experienced some kind of trauma in their lives. As the children of rich or successful people can sometimes demonstrate, the path without hurdles is often one of the most dangerous, because it saps you of the motivation needed to achieve things.

By contrast, the experience of being hurt, abandoned or growing up poor can be one of the greatest drivers for finding success. It's well established that children who have either lost or been let down by a parent have a strong tendency to go on to have highly successful careers. The author Malcolm Gladwell has classed these people as the 'eminent orphans': those who turned the trauma of losing a parent into the motivation to lead a disproportionately successful life. Of America's forty-five presidents, a dozen – from George Washington to Barack Obama – saw their father die at a young age, while an estimated two-thirds of UK prime ministers between the beginning of the nineteenth century and the beginning of the Second World War lost a parent before the age of sixteen. Other studies have linked the early death of a parent to success in fields from science to poetry.

Why are those who experience this sort of loss disposed to become more creative, determined, ambitious and, ultimately, successful? Independence must be a part of it. When, as a child, you lose part of the protective circle around you, it demands more of you and toughens you as a result. When you have to adapt and grow up early, in most cases you do just that. It's the life equivalent of having the stabilizers taken off your bike before you have properly learned to ride it, or having the inflatable armbands removed at the swimming pool. Through necessity, you learn to stay on the bike and to keep your head above water.

These things are not exclusive to those who have suffered the early death of a parent. You do not need to have been bereaved or orphaned in childhood to understand what abandonment feels like, or be thrust into a position where you have to take responsibility at an earlier age than is natural. The same is true of those whose parents are often absent through work or personal problems with drugs or alcohol; for those who are left in a position where they have to care for a sick or ill parent; and for others who become estranged from their families. It's also true for those who grow up poor, and of whom little is expected in life; or for others who are rejected, criticized or abused by an authority figure.

The point is, such an experience leaves you as someone burning to prove your point, to the parent who rejected or abandoned you, to the teacher who said you would never amount to anything, or to the other kids at school who bullied or abused you. There is no more powerful motivator in life than wanting to prove someone or something wrong.

Once they have taken on the trappings of success, it can be hard to see that people with huge fortunes or incredible achievements in life could ever have been any other way. But the most important version of that person isn't the one who drives a Bentley, has buildings named after them and gets their picture in the paper every week. Instead, it's the child who was rejected, abandoned or racially abused. An experience like that never leaves you and it provides a motivation that, however successful you become, never stops driving you on.

They relentlessly and obsessively pursue objectives

When an athlete wins a gold medal, or breaks a world record, do they usually retire afterwards, having achieved the pinnacle of their sport?

Unless age or injury is a factor, the answer will generally be no. Because among the successful, achieving one thing simply makes you want to achieve more. Why stop at one gold medal when you could be a multiple champion and break more records, including your own? For elite footballers, a league title is one thing, but what about the Champions League, the World Cup, the Ballon d'Or? There is always something more to aspire to – in sport, business or any other pursuit you could name. The most successful people are those who see achievements not as end points but staging posts, pointing not towards the sun lounger but the next big challenge. I am well known for not celebrating business deals, as I have normally already moved on to the next one!

That is the relentlessness which typifies successful people. It's partly about your ambitions and how these are constantly resetting themselves and growing in scale. It's also about your approach to everyday life and work. If, like every successful person, you are driven by a big picture you are trying to achieve, this becomes the dominant feature in your life. A big picture doesn't take holidays or get locked in your desk drawer over the weekend. It is always there, demanding attention and action, an itch that needs to be constantly scratched. For that reason, elite athletes don't stop training because it's a bank holiday (the decathlete Daley Thompson was famous for training twice on Christmas Day, on the basis that his competitors would be having a day off or doing one session at the most); novelists don't stop taking in the world around them and making notes when they go away; and entrepreneurs don't stop thinking about their businesses – well, they don't stop thinking about them at all, to be honest.

One of my closest friends, Pawan Kenth, runs a very successful corporate-wear business and was relentless in his pursuit of customers, never going anywhere – a restaurant, a gym, even a nightclub – without trying to sell some kind of product to the people running it. He was permanently looking for customers and sales opportunities, night and day. He has gone on to diversify into housing and hospitality, with the same relentless approach and success. I am guilty of the same. I can't walk down a high street, anywhere in the world, without clocking the 'for sale' boards and mentally sizing up the possible investment opportunities. My radar is always up, and I am never truly switched off from eyeing up the market around me, even if I would never actually invest in it.

To be successful, you need that level of obsession with your big picture. Defining achievements don't just fall into your lap. They have to be earned through relentless hard work, self-improvement and opportunism. To someone with a deeply rooted big picture, this comes naturally. It is the thing that matters above all to you in life, and so you think nothing of organizing your entire life around it. You need that relentlessness to really succeed, and you need the motivation to be strong enough to sustain it.

They are not afraid of change

Most people are afraid of change. They're not sure if they, or their business, used to thriving in a particular set of circumstances, will be able to repeat the trick when conditions change. Many crave a sense of certainty that they can fall back on when times get tough.

To know that this is the case, you only have to look at how change in the business world is generally reported in the media and debated within industry. We hear almost nothing but doom about the death of the high street, or the rise of robots, with far less acknowledgement of the opportunities these changes will create. The prevailing culture is one that shouts loudly about shops closing and jobs being lost, and pays scant attention to the different tenants that will occupy those properties, and the new jobs that technology will create in its wake.

Successful people, and companies, swim against this tide. They recognize that change is a law of life, and that as well as destroying some parts of the status quo, it inevitably also opens new doors for those rational enough to see them.

More than that, they recognize that moments of change are actually the most exciting times, when you can move fastest and furthest in markets that are full of fear and deficient in common sense. There is a saying that **'you should never waste a crisis'**, and every entrepreneur is the embodiment of that philosophy. They see change not as something to survive – keeping your head down in the storm – but a moment to capitalize and make bold moves.

Change equals opportunity because you know others will be ducking for cover and divesting assets. That means the field is open, and potentially valuable investments are there for the taking at cut prices.

Psychologists use something called the Rorschach test for determining aspects of a patient's personality: these are paintings made up of ambiguous ink blots that can be interpreted in a wide variety of different ways, depending on your perspective. It is thought by some to provide an insight into how people's minds work and how they process information. Moments of change are a Rorschach test that determine those who have the mentality for success. The evidence is the same – it is what people choose to see that differs. Where some perceive danger and destruction, the successful eye opportunity. What you see determines how you respond. Successful people are those who never spot a change without seeing an opportunity within it.

They are not easily impressed, and don't suffer fools, timewasters or bullshitters

An essential attribute of most successful people I know is their scepticism. That might sound at odds with the positivity I discussed earlier in the chapter, but the two actually go hand in hand. Being positive about the opportunities in front of you, and your own ability to capitalize on them, does not mean you have to be wide-eyed about everything and everyone that crosses your path.

In fact, it is very important that you match an inner positivity with an outward scepticism, especially when it comes to people. The world is full of chancers, frauds and those looking to take you for a ride. Funnily enough, you encounter a lot more of them once you have had some success and made a bit of money. Suddenly you are in demand in a way that was never previously the case. Your phone rings and people come knocking on your door to seek advice, offer deals and solicit your involvement in all number of different schemes.

Some of these will be genuine opportunities. I have benefited in all sorts of ways from being involved in advisory roles with organizations.

You need to be open to the world around you, establishing a profile that allows you to build the sort of professional network that is part and parcel of success.

But for every one of these instances, there are plenty of so-called opportunities that are somewhere on a scale between wasting your time and actively seeking to exploit your credibility and reputation. These are the conversations that successful people learn to filter out and very quickly withdraw themselves from. You can't shut yourself off from the world because you fear being taken for a ride, but nor can you entertain those who are simply trying it on. Being unimpressed with people, and generally assuming that people won't live up to their billing, is a useful filter for helping to ensure that, when you do decide to do business with or hire someone, they have surmounted a high bar.

In the end, the most valuable commodity for all of us is time. Learning how to use yours is one of the most important skills, and successful people are ruthlessly efficient in dedicating time towards jobs that both need doing, and where their intervention can make a difference. That means having a keen instinct for when something isn't as it seems, and keeping timewasters and bullshitters at bay. It also means surrounding yourself with capable, trustworthy and reliable people who know your mind and will help protect you from these situations. No one builds a successful business without being an excellent judge of character, capable of filtering out the opportunists and identifying the outstanding. That's why, if you want to know what category someone falls into, a good place to start is to look at the people they surround themselves with: the company they keep. That usually tells you everything you need to know.

Most have money in their head, not in their hearts

If I think of the successful entrepreneurs I know, there is a difference between those who have done quite well for themselves – enough to own a few houses and go on holiday whenever and wherever they want – and others whose wealth and success is on another level: in the hundreds of millions rather than single figures.

The ones who think, talk and worry about money aren't those who have made the most. That isn't just because of the simple fact that they have enough not to worry. You could probably say that of all the people I am talking about. The difference is in the attitude towards money. The highest achievers are also usually the most generous, benevolent and giving of their time and resources.

As I said in the previous chapter, you don't become successful by setting out to make money. That just isn't your end goal, which is instead about what the money enables you to do. The most successful people really live up to this. They treat business as business, and money as money: their emotional investment is not in the making of money or the building of a business per se, but in fulfilling their big picture.

That attitude translates into how successful people think about and run their businesses. They are rational and not emotional in their decision-making and professional relationships. They do not live and die with every fluctuation of the business or market, and are happy to lose some battles as long as they remain on track to win the war, which is achieving their big picture.

This matters because it's easy to let personal feelings get in the way of good business. You can't be successful if you keep falling out with your business partners or associates. That tends to happen when people get too personal in business conversations and let their emotions cloud their judgement.

For example, one of my interests outside of property is a restaurant business, Asha's (which is the best curry house in the UK). I run it alongside one of my oldest friends, Pawan Kenth (the corporate-wear king), someone I have known for over thirty years. The nature of co-owning a business is that you often need to have very direct conversations, where you are honest about each other's failings and the errors that have been made. You can't have that kind of no-holds-barred dialogue if you are forever trying to soften the blow and worried about how your friend might react. For the two of us it works, because we are able to treat business as business, and friendship as friendship, and not let one intrude on the other.

The people who don't succeed are those who take professional criticism personally and get too emotional about their work. By contrast, successful people excel at separating the two. They are unashamedly direct in the way they go about their business dealings and perfectly capable (most of the time!) of maintaining a friendly personal relationship with someone they slug it out with in the business context. To achieve that separation you need to have money in your head, not your heart. If you are too emotionally invested in what should be objective business decisions and conversations, you will lack the clarity needed to make the right calls. The most successful people never forget that it is just business, and needs to be treated accordingly.

Glass ceilings don't exist for them

As I discussed earlier, one of the great enemies of success is the limiting belief: the self-imposed barrier that people put in front of themselves, saying I can't possibly hope to achieve this, compete with them or aspire to that.

The most successful people are those who have escaped these limiting beliefs. That is because they have an essential positivity, the confidence that they are capable of achieving whatever goals they set themselves, and overcoming almost any obstacles that fall in their path.

It's for that reason that you generally won't find successful people who talk about having 'smashed the glass ceiling'. In their mind, it never really existed. The entrepreneurial mindset says that nothing is stopping you, the field is open and you can rise as high as your skills and hard work will take you.

By contrast, the glass-ceiling mentality is one held by people who feel that they haven't achieved what they wanted to, and want to find something to blame. They have risen as high as society allowed them to, the argument goes. It wasn't their fault that they couldn't go any further.

But the truth is that while structural racism, sexism and other forms of prejudice undoubtedly exist in society, the glass ceiling only really exists in the minds of those who for whatever reason have failed to live up to their own hopes or expectations. It is one of the greatest and most dangerous limiting beliefs, because it encourages whole communities to believe that success beyond a certain level is simply not an option for them.

That is as damaging as it is untrue. If it were the case, no immigrant group would ever do what the vast majority have done, and achieve disproportionate social and economic mobility. Had you asked the glass-ceiling crowd in the 1970s what the prospects were for an Asian kid like me, I imagine they would have set the bar pretty low.

If you ever believed in the glass ceiling, you would never achieve much at all. Successful people don't harbour that belief – in fact it doesn't even really occur to them. And that is why they succeed.

They learn from high achievers and establish a network of like-minded friends and associates

There is a herd instinct in people that means we tend to hang around with others like us: parents socialize with other parents, property people with other property people, neighbours with other neighbours. You have interests, experiences and frustrations in common: stories to share and news to pass on.

Successful people are no different. They want to surround themselves with like minds, those who aren't going to try to exploit them in some way, but rather will look out for them. You want a sense of recognition from peers, and a sense of belonging with others like you.

Beyond that, the most important thing about a network is your ability to learn from others around you. A network isn't just about having direct peers who are your equal. Successful people will also seek out people who are older, more experienced and more accomplished than them, those from whom they can learn.

As a kid I played football with those who were older than me, because I knew it helped me to get better. Learning about business is essentially no different. You identify those who have built the kind of thing you want to build, and they become either your role model, or if you are lucky, your mentor. My role model, Roy Richardson, taught me to be fair, caring and ambitious at the same time as being tough and standing up to institutions and the establishment. He also taught me how to bring through the next generations.

Those role models will change over time as your business and your big picture evolve. In recent years, having built up a business of a certain size, and with my son and nephews now making their way in the industry, my attention has turned to what the company will become after I am gone. My ambition isn't just for what I can build myself, but for the legacy that I will leave.

That means my role models are family businesses that have come from nothing and grown and thrived over many generations – companies like Caledonia, which has been in the Cayzer family since it was founded in the 1870s. Knowing that a business like that exists helps give you confidence that not every company has to go bust or lose its way after a couple of generations. And if you can get to know them and hear how they have done it first hand, even better. Reading is one thing, but being able to talk with people and ask questions is the best kind of learning.

Successful people are relentless in their ambition, continually expanding the horizons of their big picture and adding new detail. A network is an essential part of how you do that, and successful people grow and evolve theirs in the same way as they do their company. They realize that there is always another, higher level of achievement to aspire to, and that one of the bridges towards it is in getting to know the people who have already made it and being able to ask them how.

They regularly step out of their comfort zones

'Never settle, create the life you deserve to live and help others do the same.'

PAUL BASSI CBE

Now I'm into the second half of my fifties, I know more and more people who have taken early retirement in one form or another. These are often people who have been quite successful, reached a point where they own the things they want to own and can afford a lifestyle they enjoy. They've got a pension pot, their kids have grown up and they feel like it's time to put their feet up and enjoy the fruits of their hard work.

Except the reality of retirement is often very different from the dream of sandy beaches, rounds of golf several times a week and holidays whenever you want them. While you gain the benefits of freedom from routine and endless leisure time, you have also lost something fundamental: the purpose that your working life gave you, and the challenges it threw up to keep you sharp.

It is entirely possible to enjoy a retirement that continues to stretch and energize you. The former US President Jimmy Carter, at the age of ninety-four, still puts on a hard hat and overalls to help build houses as part of his Habitat for Humanity project. But for many, retirement means less stimulation rather than more, and the gradual settling into a life of relaxation.

In other words, it is a passport to that most dangerous of places in any life: the comfort zone. This is something people often think they want, but never actually enjoy when they get there. You might crave the certainty it appears to offer, but you will quickly find that it's actually quite an uncomfortable place to be. Nothing changes, nothing happens and there is little left to excite or surprise you. The comfort zone is not a good place to spend any length of time. It's a recipe for one part complacency, and another anxiety about what you are missing out on beyond your bubble, all topped off with the creeping feeling of unfulfilled potential.

Because they are relentless, truly successful people recognize the truth in the assertion by Neale Donald Walsch, that **'life begins at the end of your comfort zone'**. They are deaf to its siren song, and actively seek out the uncertainty and the adrenaline hit of new experiences and higher bars to clear.

One friend who retired a decade ago, at the age of fifty-five, is now getting back into business. He did all the things you would expect a retired, relatively wealthy person to do, but found limited fulfilment in any of them. Only by coming back to work, launching a new venture and getting out of the comfort zone of retirement is he now finding what he was looking for all along: a balanced and healthy lifestyle, with the opportunity for continuous Kaizen.

The comfort zone is an unhealthy place, at any stage in life. Being in it for too long is a form of living death, where you exist but achieve little that is meaningful to you. Getting out of the comfort zone is actively medicinal, providing the purpose, focus and whiff of danger that we all need to perform at our best. That is why you will never encounter a successful person who is comfortable resting on their laurels. The Microsoft founder Bill Gates put it best when he said, '**if I'd had some set idea of a finish line, don't you think I would have crossed it years ago?**' The most successful are never done, and the idea of having 'made it' simply doesn't exist. They carry on, towards the next thing and away from the dangerous complacency of the comfort zone.

How they do anything is how they do everything

The smallest thing can make a big difference in how we see people and judge their character. Were they on time for the meeting? Did they say thank you to the person who held a door open for them? Did they switch off the lights as the last person to leave the room? Did they pay proper attention to someone who was talking to them, or were they looking at their phone the whole time?

This isn't just human instinct. These small indicators tell us a lot about a person. Behaviour travels across all aspects of life. If you're slovenly in your personal habits, you're unlikely to be meticulous in how you go about business. If you're too lazy to go to the gym and keep to an agreed fitness schedule, you're probably not going to be putting in the extra hours needed at work. And if you're discourteous or impolite to people when you think others aren't looking, eventually that is going to seep into your professional relationships too, however hard you might try to conceal it.

There are no coincidences in people's behaviour. How we do anything is how we do everything. There aren't different versions of ourselves we can switch on and off, like swapping a tracksuit for a two-piece suit.

The most successful people I know are also those who are the most disciplined, meticulous and polite in how they go about every part of their life. They smile, say thank you, hold doors open and are thoughtful to those around them, not just their peers. They never miss a visit to the gym and they are never late for a meeting. If they say they will do something, then they always follow through as promised. There are never excuses for a deadline slipping or a promise not being kept. And you will never hear through the grapevine that they have bad-mouthed you to someone else. (This is always a mistake. I once attended a party when, after learning that I worked in property in West Bromwich, someone said that he knew the scene there a bit, and that I should make sure to avoid this guy called Paul Bassi, who was apparently very hard to get along with.)

Successful people don't observe some imaginary divide between their personal and professional lives. They demonstrate the same habits and behaviours whether it's about keeping fit or landing their next major deal.

The golfer Gary Player once said that, **'The more I practise, the luckier I seem to get.'** There is an important life lesson in that. You have to behave like a successful person throughout your life, if you want to achieve your big picture. You can't behave like a successful person at work and be a complete slob at home. Those two personas can't coexist: you are one or the other.

It's for the same reason that successful people are generally highly competitive personalities and take their sporting and social pursuits as seriously as their work. You won't find someone who pursues every last scrap of value in a negotiation on a Friday, then is satisfied to jog around at the back of the field, or go for a gentle kickabout, on Saturday. If you have a desperate need to win in one area of life, it's going to be the same across your whole life.

Successful people do even the smallest things with the same discipline, relentlessness and focus as those which seem to be the most important. For them, the distinction simply doesn't exist.

They have a thick skin

Successful people aren't just good at achieving their ambitions; they also learn to deal with the challenges that success brings with it.

One of the most frequent of these challenges is having to deal with the criticism, negativity and envy of others. Success means visibility, and very quickly you find yourself becoming a bit of a public dartboard for criticism. This can come from friends or family, who say that you've changed and don't give them the time of day anymore (often disregarding the reality that, in their own way, their life has got just as busy as yours, and it's a two-way street). It can be your competitors, who are trying in various ways to undermine you. Or it can be those who, because you are in the public eye, feel like they have the right to have a go at you. Americans call this class of critics the peanut gallery, referring to the cheap seats in twentieth-century vaudeville theatres, where people went to heckle and throw things at the performers. That is one of the realities of becoming successful: like it or not, you are on the stage and have in some way become public property. No surprise, therefore, that some of the richest and most successful people I know do everything they can to maintain their privacy and avoid exactly this kind of attention.

Often you know the criticism to be unfair or based on untrue assumptions. People will sometimes say to me that they never stop seeing my name in the paper, even though I do almost no proactive publicity other than when the business is reporting its results. But it's the impression that counts, and this often runs ahead of the facts. People who have never met you form strong ideas about you, and then have no hesitation in sharing them with you if your paths eventually cross. There is also the reality that no good deed goes unpunished. The school that my charitable trust helps fund in West Bromwich, one of the things about which I am most proud, has been the subject of criticism from people who say that it's elitist and only meets the needs of a few hundred pupils, when there are so many in need. To which I say, isn't it better to have helped some, who can then influence others, than none at all?

Successful people don't let this low hum of criticism affect them. They are focused on their own big picture, not what other people think. They know that the respect of those you work with and have around you is worth much more than the opinion of the many who have never met you. And they don't let the heckles from the peanut gallery distract their focus or affect them in any meaningful way.

In fact, these things can in their own way be something of a source of strength. I like to think there is almost something regal about being ill-spoken of when you are doing well. It's another reminder that you're succeeding. In the property industry, there is a tendency for successful people to be more respected than they are liked. If you double your money on a smart investment in a handful of years, you're not just doing well for yourself, but showing up the fact that others missed out on the same opportunity. People might not like you for it, but they do respect you for having the bravery to take on the risk.

When the brickbats start flying, you need to remember what you set out to achieve in the first place. It's about the big picture, not a popularity contest in which you wanted everyone to support you. If you are seeking the approval and thanks of others for the work you are doing, then you're probably in the wrong job and reading the wrong book. I see my job as making money for my shareholders and my staff, and then using some of that to invest back in our community, as we do through the school and other charitable interests. If other people want to criticize me for that, then that's fine – but I don't care and I'm not listening. You can't keep the whole world happy and it's a waste of time responding to every barb that gets thrown your way.

Success in business will earn you plenty of critics. Learn to relish them, because they are a sign that you are doing well enough to be worth attacking. Just as rats flee a sinking ship, critics try to board one that is going places. The time to worry is when they stop paying any attention to you at all.

They take a long-term view

A lot of the attributes I've discussed in this chapter will feel like they are about the here and now. And it's true, successful people are focused and relentless about seizing opportunities: looking for progress each and every day. But that doesn't mean they expect success to happen quickly.

In fact, the most successful people are those who recognize that the really big plays – deals that run into tens of millions, major acquisitions or significant expansions – are things that happen on a timescale not of months or even years, but often decades. There is so much groundwork you need to do to be ready for that moment, putting the necessary foundations in place, that there is simply no way of rushing it.

It's the same outside of business. Olympic athletes are typically those who have trained for years and years, often since early childhood, to get to the starting line. Some of the world's most famous books were years in the writing. Real, meaningful success never comes quickly.

It's well established that the most successful businesses take a long-term view. According to a McKinsey study of US public companies between 2001 and 2015, those that were long-term in their thinking saw revenue growth that was 47% faster, earnings that were 36% higher and an average increase in market capitalization $7bn above that of short-term competitors.

The advice I tend to give to young people who approach me is 'Don't rush it.' It's true that all young men and women are in a hurry, but it's also the wrong approach. No meaningfully successful person has the mentality of the get-rich-quick scheme. They understand the realities of how you create long-term value, and know that you often won't see the real dividend of your hard work until many years later. Rates of return in business are not linear: you don't get out exactly what you put in, at the time you are investing. You have to keep on building and evolving a company that is going to be valuable, and deliver the real return for you when both the business and the market are ready. You can no more short-cut this process than you can expect to take a cake out of the oven and eat it before it is properly baked.

I've never bought a business or property on the assumption that I could sell it quickly. Some will have a shorter turnaround and lifecycle than others, but you always have to be willing to both put the work in and wait for the right moment before cashing in. Some investments are extremely long-term in their outlook. About twenty years ago, I bought 100 acres of land that was adjacent to existing housing, but prohibited from development as part of the green belt. At the time of writing, that still stands, but I am convinced that – with the ongoing housing shortage – eventually planning permission will be granted for that land, and what was bought for a few thousand pounds per acre, will be worth in the region of half a million or even a million per acre. Whether that happens in my lifetime or for the next generation doesn't really matter. In the long term, even if it is the *very* long term, that is going to be an excellent investment.

I believe you can't expect to be successful unless you understand how successful people behave – the attitudes, character traits and good habits that unite a diverse group of people across business, sport, the arts and public service.

Some of the things I have mentioned are simply common threads I have observed among the successful people I know: from having been let down or abandoned by a parent to having excelled at sport. But many are behaviours that you need to learn from and replicate if you are going to be successful in your chosen field. You need to be positive, relentless and stay well clear of your comfort zone. You can't be someone who offers excuses, or who accepts them from the people around you: it always has to be about the solution, not the problem – what happens next. And you need to combine that relentless approach to immediate challenges with a patience which accepts that success does not happen fast, and that the most meaningful rewards are those reaped over the long term.

Perhaps most importantly of all, you need to understand that being successful isn't a persona you inhabit, but a life you have to live. The most successful people I know do the least important thing with the same attitude and approach as the most important. How they do anything is how they do everything.

You can't have the things you want – longevity, material fulfilment, family happiness – without being willing to dig deep and put the work in. It's not about following some of the rules and habits here, and hoping for the best. It's about embodying all of them: living the whole life, not just acting out a few parts. And that is where the obsessive focus comes in. Your big picture needs to be meaningful enough to warrant all of this hard work and focus. Either it is worth dedicating your life towards, or none of this is ever going to happen.

Be in no doubt – there are no accidents when it comes to success. Those who achieve it have a clear plan and a rigorous approach to achieving it. Success happens through repeated, long-term commitment to the big picture, not through a whim and some lucky breaks. And it arises through the establishment of good habits, ones which repeat and reflect across your whole life. You need to study and understand successful people to understand that their achievements are only possible through a huge investment of positivity, focus and stamina. In other words, they succeed through being relentless.

4

Planning for success

If you fail to plan, you are planning to fail.
BENJAMIN FRANKLIN

So far we've looked at how to understand success, and the traits that unite and define the most successful people in life. Let's now shift the focus to you: how can you start to put these lessons into practice, and plot a path to success in your own life and chosen career?

It all starts with planning and having a clear idea of where you want to get to. You need to begin, as they say, at the end.

Most of us have sat in a job interview and been asked where we see ourselves in five or ten years' time. It's often a question that will be answered by talking about what kind of job you want to have by then, or it might be about family, or where you hope to be living.

The question of your future destination is the fundamental one for anyone who wants to be successful in their life. But you need to expand the time horizon. It's not just about a few years or a decade away. You need to ask the question about your whole life, or at least to think in decades.

In other words, you need to set yourself a big picture. In this chapter, I want to take you through how that is done, and how then to work towards it. Before we get to any of the specifics about how to build a business or a property portfolio, you need to be clear on your big picture: what will all of this help you achieve?

I'll start by sharing mine with you. It's my 101st birthday. I'm having a party, surrounded by all of my family: children, grandchildren, maybe even great-grandchildren, all or most will be highly educated and successful in their chosen fields and the family name and business will represent integrity, trust, respect and honesty. The next generations will have taken on substantial and diverse businesses, which will be thriving even more than they did before. When I get there – to 21 March 2063 – with all the people and things I want with me, then I know everything else will have been successful. I will have achieved everything I ever wanted. My greatest pride and joy will be to have planted trees under whose shade I may never sit.

That 101st birthday party is my big picture because it encompasses everything I have ever wanted to achieve: the building of a multidisciplinary property business, one that I will pass on to the next generation of my family to grow and evolve even further; a family I love and am proud of, whose success I have helped to ensure; and all the material things I ever wanted and didn't have as the son of immigrants in the 1960s and 1970s.

It's a big picture that has been driven by things I wanted – the business, the thriving family, the material things – but also something I feared: the threat of losing it all, going back to where I started and to the life my parents lived. The things you want keep you looking forwards, and those you fear are essential to making sure you stay hungry and focused.

I've had that big picture written down in a book for over thirty years, the same book in which I write down and track my goals every year. It stays there, reminding me what all of this is about and what I am working towards.

This planning is an essential part of how I have lived my life ever since my early twenties. Just as there are no real coincidences in life, I believe there is no successful person who didn't plan for it. You have to know where you are going (the big picture) and to work out the steps that are going to get you there (the goals). While not every successful person documents their ambitions like this, they all have a plan and a big picture. Incidentally, people who do document their planning are statistically more likely to achieve their goals and to a greater scale.

The importance of planning is universal, but different people approach it in different ways. I am going to share my method with you, one which offers a straightforward and rigorous approach to ensuring you set a clear path and stick to it, assessing your progress continuously as you go. Here's how it works.

Set a big picture

Without a destination you can't set a route, so there is no point trying to set goals without a clear understanding of what they are contributing towards – and where they are taking you.

Some people find this straightforward. They know they want to own three houses in three countries, become CEO of a public company, be a bestselling novelist, an award-winning heart surgeon or simply raise and look after a family they love. If you have that certainty and confidence, that's a great start.

But if you don't, don't worry. Articulating what you really want from life is not easy, and some find it intimidating. Others claim that they simply don't have big ambitions at all. This last claim is never true. Everyone has things they want to achieve and dreams they harbour, however secretly. The problem is that lots of us are conditioned by society to think we need to conform to other people's idea of what a good life looks like; and many of us also believe our ambitions to be unrealistic or even frivolous. A lot of people are scared and doubt themselves, to the point of inaction.

You have to lose that mentality if you are going to identify and establish a big picture. Forget self-deprecation, forget putting yourself down and forget your inhibitions about what is and isn't possible. Just focus on what it is you actually want.

The first step towards achieving a life ambition really is to admit that you have one. This can be one of the hardest parts. But unless you cross this hurdle, you are never going to get any further. So try to get comfortable with the idea. Think what it might feel like, what your days would look like, who will be around you and what they will say. Try to visualize what it will be like, and enjoy the feeling. Let yourself dream a little about what that future could be. Remember that this is *your* big picture: not what your mum wants you to do, or what you think other people will find impressive. It's the thing that's personal and important to you, and it doesn't matter in the least whether others would see it the same way.

If you can't even get to that point, then you need to find a way to unblock yourself. You have to get away from the clutter and concerns of your everyday and find some free mental space that will enable you to look forward and visualize. For some people this might mean pouring a few large whiskies; others might prefer a long walk or to do something they enjoy but don't normally get the chance to do. Whatever it is, make sure it's something that sits outside your daily routine, comes without distractions and allows you free space to think. And bring a pad. Let yourself daydream a bit and write down what comes to you: things you want, ambitions you've harboured, dreams you had as a kid but have pushed to one side. Get it all down on paper and then, the next day, go back over it. In those jottings you should have the basis of what will become your big picture. For some with institutionalized blockage, it may take a few weeks, but stick at it: this process will transform you.

I say write it down, but a big picture shouldn't be your personal version of *War and Peace*. It could just as easily be a handful of sentences. What matters at this stage is not the extent of the detail but the breadth of the vision. The big picture has to be something that is going to be worthy of all your blood, sweat and tears to achieve, and something big enough that it will take decades to get there. It's a life's work in the making: your life's work.

It should be something you can see yourself doing – so if you can't imagine walking on Mars, that's probably not going to happen – but it shouldn't be easy or accessible. It needs to be at the limits of your world: a place you will be able to reach, but one that at the outset feels distant and out of reach. That balance between being realistic and challenging is key.

Take time over your big picture, because more than anything else I will talk about, it is what really matters. Everything else is really a means to this end: the place you want your life to take you. But don't put off the discipline of working it out and writing it down. If you delay doing this, nothing else you do is going to be nearly as productive as it could be. I believe almost all of us have a big picture that exists somewhere in our heads, even if it's pretty foggy, or something we deny ourselves. The trick is to tease it out, let it breathe and be honest about what you really want.

Once you have it, write it down and file it away for now – you will visit it on a regular basis. And give yourself a pat on the back. You've already taken the most important step.

1. Work out the roadmap

A big picture is your starting point on the road to success, but functionally it's your destination. Once it's clear in your mind and written down, you need to start plotting a route that is going to get you there.

At this stage, your big picture is going to be one of broad brushstrokes. You know where you want to end up, but not how you are going to get there. You won't be able to summon all the detail at this stage, but you can break down the journey from A to B into the steps you see in front of you. Where do you need to be in one year, to build a platform to where you can end up in ten years? What are the different things you need to achieve: developing experience, achieving qualifications, nurturing a network? You should make a list of all the things you are going to need and the different stages you are going to have to go through.

Let's say you are someone working as a chef, and your big picture is that you want to eventually own a number of restaurants. My first questions to you would be about the vision: what kind of restaurants, for what customers, in what cities or countries? Then we need to look at you: how you will develop and the skills you will need to acquire. Are you already running a restaurant kitchen, and if not, how can you get to that point and acquire that experience? How are you going to fund the venture and who is going to run the business side of things? What else will you need to learn under someone else's mentorship before striking out on your own? And do you already have someone you would consider a mentor who can teach you? If it's going to be a chain or group of restaurants, at what point will you open your second, and what role will you then assume? Will they be carbon copies of each other or complementary offerings? How will you build a team capable of delivering on your vision and maintaining quality across the board?

You start mapping your way from now to the fulfilment of your big picture by setting yourself the questions that will get you there: all the stages of evolution, the things that will need to be achieved and the problems that will have to be solved. For as far as you can see ahead, you need to have a plan.

Not all of these questions will be able to be answered at the word go, but you still need to be thinking about them, and you need to understand how to work your way towards the answers. In the short term that might be about developing your own skills and experience. In the medium term it's going to involve building up a network of people who will be sources of funding, ideas and potential business partnership. And in the long term it's going to entail building the team and operation that you will need to make your big picture a reality.

You need an awareness of all these things at the outset, even if you don't yet know how all of them are going to happen. And you need to start plotting it as a timeline and a series of goals: this allows me to do that; I need to have achieved this one thing before I can hope to attack another. This isn't *Star Trek* and there are no quantum leaps. Your only route is through a long series of small steps, ones that build on each other and over time make the future steps possible. Break down the roadmap towards your big picture into a series of manageable goals, and work out how one thing brings you in range of the next. Like scrambling up a rock-face, you are always looking for your next foothold.

This timeline is the starting point. But it would be a mistake to think of planning as something that happens only at the outset of your big picture. Planning should happen continuously, and is one of the most important investments of time a person can make. Here's how I suggest going about it.

2. Set goals that pass the acid tests

You might assume that, at the age of fifty-six, with over three decades of business experience behind me, I don't really need to plan out my goals and my year in any organized way. But you'd be wrong. I have been writing down my goals in the same file for over thirty years, and I take it just as seriously now as I did then. Indeed, I have more goals and boxes to tick today than ever before.

Unless you set specific goals, you are never going to achieve the things you want. For the vast majority of us, unless goals are written down they don't mean anything. There's a reason that between 80%

and 90% of New Year's resolutions are estimated to come to nothing. People make vague promises to themselves, but nothing is committed to or formalized, and after a few weeks of good intentions, old habits reassert themselves. It's hard to emphasize enough how important it is to actually write down your goals. This seems obvious to those of us who do it, but never occurs to many people. Don't just take my word for it. According to a Harvard Business School study conducted with the class of 1979, the 3% of alumni who focused on writing down their goals out-earned the other 97% by a factor of ten in the decade after graduation.

Unless you go through the discipline of setting goals in a careful and thorough way, they aren't going to happen. My approach is to start each year with a written list of goals I plan to achieve within the next twelve months. I will start formulating these each November and reassess them on a semi-regular basis throughout the year. They will include everything from things I want to achieve within the business, to the holidays I want to take, and personal development goals (like going to the gym three times a week, or learning Spanish). At the top of each year's page I have written down my big picture: the 101st birthday. That's a constant reminder that these goals aren't a random list of things I want to achieve, but building blocks towards the most important ambition in my life.

When I'm setting goals, I weigh the things in my head against four 'acid tests', ones that help determine whether it is worth including or not. These are worth recounting in detail, as they are fundamental to the discipline of effective goal-setting and planning. The four tests, necessary components of every single goal you set, are:

Is it detailed?

Whenever I have review or performance meetings with people who work for me, I will always ask them about their goals beyond work and the business. Often you hear things like 'I want to buy a new car.' To which my question is always, 'What car?' Some people can tell you every last detail, from the calibre of the engine to the colour of the paintwork and the leather on the seats. Others just shrug: they haven't really thought about it. Can you guess who is going to be driving a new car at Christmas?

Detail is so important to goal-setting because you have to be able to imagine something if you're going to achieve it. Remember the house I knew I wanted at the age of twenty-two, and now live in? Thirty-five years ago, I didn't just know that it was going to be a big house. I knew what the architecture should be, and how the drive would look. I could picture the whole thing in my mind.

You need to be able to do the same, not just for your big picture but for every single small goal you are setting. Maybe you're someone who wants to get into the habit of reading more. But what books, how many and how often? Or you might want to travel more adventurously. You'll only do that if you know the countries, cities and specific sites you want to visit.

Again, there are no accidents in who does and doesn't succeed. Achievement of the things you want follows from effective planning for them. That all starts with having a clear vision of what you want. Not a vague aspiration, not an idle hope – but a detailed idea, from which a tangible plan can follow. Without that detail, you don't really know what you want to achieve, and the game is lost before it's even started.

Is it challenging?

Goals should be about helping you get better and achieve the things you want. A goal isn't something you can accomplish without any serious effort. It needs to be a target that helps you adapt, improve and change as a person.

That means there needs to be an element of challenge about your goals. There's no point saying you want to lose weight and get fitter, and then setting a target of losing one or two pounds. That isn't enough of an objective to really motivate you, or to inspire a change in habits.

You want to make your goals a little bit intimidating, things you're not completely sure you will be able to achieve. Because those are the only ones actually worth achieving. They prove to you that you are capable of more than you realize or expect. They create a sense of achievement and most importantly they build confidence, without which very little of meaning can be accomplished. A goal that isn't sufficiently challenging will either be achieved so easily that it doesn't feel worthwhile, or not prove sufficiently motivating to be tackled at all.

If you want to get more confident, then be prepared to challenge yourself. Always set the bar just a little bit higher than you are comfortable with. Without this kind of challenge, you have neither the motivation to get going in the first place, nor the sense of achievement at what you eventually accomplish.

Is it realistic?

At the same time as challenging yourself with goals, you also need to be realistic. If I've not done any kind of fitness training in years, it's unlikely that I will immediately start going to the gym four times a week without building up to it.

Challenging goals are those which are going to stretch you and be difficult to achieve. But they are meant to be a hurdle to overcome, not a brick wall to run into. It's about improving gradually over time, not hoping for the kind of overnight transformation that doesn't happen outside the pages of glossy magazines.

Being realistic is also about how much you have time for. It's nice to have goals that cover everything from career to fitness, travel to culture, learning and so on. But there are only so many hours in the day, and there are only so many things one person can properly focus on at the same time. Be realistic about the goals you set yourself, and be sensible about how much you take on. Better a few things pursued vigorously than many which never really go anywhere. You have to be realistic about what goals you set for yourself, and how many you will be able to do justice to.

Is it desirable?

It sounds obvious, but any goal you set yourself also has to be something you really want to do. There's no point saying you want to do something because you think it's going to impress someone, or feel it's the sort of thing you ought to be doing. You have to really want it, if it's going to be worth investing the time and effort.

The truth is that it takes effort to achieve things that feel meaningful and rewarding. The instinctive, human path of least resistance is to avoid that. No one gets themselves out of a warm bed to go running at 6am, passes up a night out to sit at home and work, or puts themselves on a diet unless it's helping them to achieve something they really want. So unless you do want it, badly enough, it's just never going to happen.

In the end, things only get done when you have sufficient desire to invest the necessary effort. It's never enough for someone else to want it for you, or to be motivated by anything other than your own inner drive and purpose. When you're weighing up whether or not to set something as a goal, ask yourself, 'Do I really, really want this?' If the answer is no, then that goal is fated to fall by the wayside, as one that didn't really matter when the alarm clock rings a second time.

These 'acid tests' should be in your mind when you are setting the goals that make up the roadmap towards your big picture. But they also function as a check and balance on your progress, and if a goal is not being progressed it will always be because it has failed one or other of the tests. It might not have been desirable enough to prioritize over everything else you had going on; or it may not have been sufficiently realistic to make time for. Whatever the case, a goal will not be achieved unless it passes all the tests. And if it doesn't, it has no business being on your list in the first place.

3. Track and measure your progress

If you are serious about achieving a big picture, and the goals that contribute towards it, you have to be disciplined about keeping track of your progress. I mentioned that most New Year's resolutions have been discarded by February. That's because – even if they passed the tests I have just outlined – the majority aren't planned and pursued in an organized way. Making a promise to yourself is one thing. But actually following through requires a plan that you keep coming back to and a commitment to follow through. You need to be relentless in making sure you stay on plan at all times.

For me that means beginning every calendar year with a written list of the goals I want to achieve, and if necessary interim deadlines that will help me get towards them (so if we're going to open a new restaurant by the end of the year, we have to have got so far by the end of the first quarter, and so on).

Having that list in the first place is important – but you can't then lock it away in a drawer and hope that by December your goals will have achieved themselves. It requires an ongoing process of review to ensure you are on track and make the necessary adjustments. This is something I recommend doing on a quarterly basis. Put time in your diary to ensure you aren't disturbed. Then sit down with your list, and be honest about which goals you are on track for, and others that are falling by the wayside.

If I'm falling behind on a goal, I either get rid of it altogether (because it turned out it wasn't realistic or desirable enough), or I relegate it to the 'sausage meat' section of my book: things I still want to do, don't currently have time for and will try to return to in the next year or two. You shouldn't have goals hanging around that aren't seeing any progress. Be honest with yourself about what is and isn't proving to be realistic.

This review process can be done independently, but is much better if you find someone to act as your goal buddy. There's nothing like peer pressure to ensure you actually do the things you have committed to. It provides the extra motivation and incentive you need to put in that extra effort on the days you're wavering. Find a person who knows and understands you and who is going to be honest with you, either prodding you to take action, offering a shoulder to cry on or helping you to realize that a particular goal simply isn't going to happen this year. With a buddy, these quarterly sessions become reciprocal: you go through each other's goals together, mark and check your progress and help them to either tweak the goal or decide to abandon it for the time being. It's the best way of ensuring you are accountable about your goals, knowing that before long you will have to report on progress to someone you don't want to disappoint.

If you work in this way together over a number of years, your goal buddy becomes an important part of your big picture. You share everything from the professional to the deeply personal, provide each other with motivation or moral support and act as the independent arbiter as to when it is the time to either double down or move on. Setting goals is one thing, but having the discipline and dedication to achieve them is a lot harder. A counterpart who is in the trenches with you can make all the difference. Just as the choice of a business partner is one of the most important you will make, finding someone who is the right buddy – close enough to understand you, but with enough distance to lend perspective – can make the difference between achieving the goals you set yourself and failing to do so.

4. Take your time

All young men and women are in a hurry. The irony about being young is that you tend to behave as if time is running out, rather than stretching out endlessly ahead of you. You want everything here and now, and you're living in the moment rather than for the long term.

With a bit of age and perspective – and I'm writing this now with my sixtieth birthday on the not-too-distant horizon – you realize that there are some distinct stages in life, ones that help explain the journey towards any big picture. In its own way, each decade of your adult life is contributing towards that end; and it's worth recognizing how they all fit together, and build on each other.

In your twenties, you find a career. Despite what you might have read about teenage multimillionaires, don't worry if you feel you haven't fully arrived by twenty-five. There's plenty of time ahead. But you need to have established a career and set yourself a big picture.

In your thirties you really learn your trade: establishing a network, honing your professional skills and gaining an understanding of how your industry operates.

Your forties should be about mastering that trade. By this stage you have established a reputation and got some resources behind you. This is the time to start making the most of everything you've learned, and benefiting from everyone you have met, worked with and done business alongside.

Into your fifties, and it's time to start seeing some of the real benefits of your hard work so far. Statistically, this is the decade when your earnings will peak, with more capital to invest than before, old debt likely to have been paid off and the opportunity to take greater risks with a safety net of accumulated capital.

By your sixties, judging by my friends who have got to that point, there's a bit more time to enjoy your winnings, even as you keep a handle on your business or career. This is when you can start to give back, doing more mentoring and helping bring through the next generation.

In your seventies, you've likely stepped back from the day-to-day business or career, and have more time to give back through volunteering or charitable interests.

By the age of eighty, you can rest and chill out a bit. You've earned it.

But don't lose momentum into your nineties: there's still time to rock the dance floor and keep trying to make babies (maybe).

You can, as I intend to do, continue to work at a pace and level of activity that will allow you to add value to your organization and continue to give you the mental stimulus you enjoy and need.

And in your eleventh decade, it's the all-important 101st birthday.

Clearly this is an approximation, and there is no set formula for how any life or career will unfold. There are all sorts of variations, from people who start second careers in midlife to those who want to retire and hit the beach at the age of forty. But the important thing to understand is that your big picture is about more than the life you are currently living, the job you are currently doing and the everyday routine you follow.

It's about how all the experiences you've had and will have aggregate, over a course of years and decades. Working towards a big picture is a gradual process of accumulation, where you acquire experience, contacts, capital, reputation and a track record. You have to take your time, and to know at the outset that it is going to be a slow process. Every year will start with its own list of goals, but make sure to see those in the context of the longer term and of course the big picture.

I'm guessing that most of you are reading this because you've got something you want to achieve, whether it's a fully fleshed-out plan for a business you are about to launch, or just an itch you've been meaning to scratch but don't quite know how. The chapters that follow are going to cover all the basics on building businesses and property investing. But before you start thinking about any of that, you need to be clear about your big picture.

The big picture won't always be a dominating feature. As you tackle your yearly goals and everyday challenges, it will often become more the backdrop than something at the forefront of your mind. But it always needs to be there, as the fundamental anchor for everything in which you invest time and effort. In the same way we rush about our daily business, probably never taking the opportunity to look up at the sky, we won't always be gazing up towards our big picture. All the same, up there it remains. Once you have the big picture in place, and you've worked out at least some of the goals that are going to get you there, you need to start building the vehicle that is going to carry you. It's time to get down to business.

5

Running a successful business

Have patience. All things are difficult before they become easy.
THOMAS FULLER

The American football coach Vince Lombardi once said that the **'price of success is hard work'**. I couldn't agree more. Before you undertake any kind of business venture, you need to accept that it will be an all-consuming part of your life. You need to commit to doing things properly, not taking short cuts, and living and breathing your business every minute of the day. It is going to become a bit of an obsession and that is the only way: to be relentless. Otherwise you're not really talking about a business, but a hobby or a sideline. There's nothing wrong with that, but nobody ever achieved their big picture in life by fitting it into their spare time.

If you have a big picture and are truly dedicated to achieving it, then you need to understand the commitment you are taking on. That should not be done lightly. But if you do, and you are willing to put in the work, then the rewards can be limitless. Do it properly and it will be one hell of a ride!

You have to know what you are getting into. You also need to acknowledge some fundamental business truths that apply whatever kind of company you are trying to build, regardless of the intended size, industry and geography. Getting your head around these basics is going to save you time and trouble on the long road ahead. In this chapter I have distilled what I have learned from building my businesses over the last thirty-five years, while watching and working with others who have created and managed companies considerably larger than mine.

This isn't a menu from which I encourage you to be selective. These are the core components of creating and sustaining a robust business and you can't pick and choose. Just as successful people do everything the way they do anything, you need to cover all the right bases of attitude, approach and business practice to build a successful enterprise.

I've grouped my advice into three sections:

1 **Planning:** how to get something started, focus your business from the outset and avoid falling at the first hurdles.

2 **People:** how to build a network of contacts and a brilliant team of people around you.

3 **Delivery:** how to get things done and keep the business going (and growing) for the long term.

Bear in mind that this isn't a step-by-step guide that takes you through things like company structures, how to manage your cash flow or run a Profit and Loss. Information like that is readily accessible and well documented elsewhere. Instead, these are principles that apply to every kind of business: ways of thinking about your company and approaches you can take to maximize opportunities and avoid mistakes. It's everything I know about how to start, run and sustain a successful business, for the long term.

Planning

Know your customer

This first point is the most important of all. You would not believe how many companies stumble and fall because – for all their clever ideas, innovative products and detailed research – they didn't spend enough time getting into the mind of the customer and understanding what they want. In the end it doesn't matter how good your product is, how slick your service or how convincing your pitch – you only have a chance of success if you have matched all of that to a real customer need.

A good business knows what their customer wants right now, and provides it. A great business anticipates what they are going to need as tastes and preferences evolve, and offers it to them before they know they need it (at the perfect moment that's neither too far in advance nor too far behind competitors).

This is what unites all successful companies. They are in the mind of the customer – understanding what they think and want, how they shop, and how to turn them from a browser into a buyer, a customer into a regular and a regular into an ambassador who goes out and tells all their friends and contacts.

Companies that fail haven't built this understanding. They hit and hope, crossing their fingers that what feels like a good idea and an interesting business will intersect with what the customer wants. This is far too important a thing to leave to chance. You need to have an intuitive understanding of customers in your industry before you even think about trying to target a new proposition and launch a business.

Consider the coffee shop, one of the real growth industries on the UK high street. They are opening like wildfire as the pub industry contracts, with the total number having grown from around 10,000 in 2007 to more than 24,000 today. Mergers and acquisition activity like Coca Cola's acquisition of Costa Coffee for almost £4 billion prove that this is a sector that's running hot. Say you wanted to join this apparent gold rush. Where do you start? With the customer, of course. In a market that is becoming increasingly saturated, you need to know your customer instinctively to have a chance of surviving in a busy landscape of major brands and independents. Who exactly are you catering for? Is it morning commuters picking up a latte to go on their way into work; mums with babies who want a place to meet up; self-employed people who are going to use your shop as a bit of an office and sit with their laptop all day; ethically minded millennials who will care about where you've sourced your coffee? The list could go on. There is no one type of customer for any business like this, and in any one shop you will inevitably get a mixture, but you can't be all things to all people.

I promise that if you go into your local coffee shop it will quickly become clear whether the majority demographic is office workers on a break, mothers and babies, self-employed workers and so on. This isn't an accident. It's something you can and must plan for. Before you launch, you need to have a clear idea of what you are and who you are for. Having a view of the target customer determines everything, from where you site your shop to what you put on the shelves and how you promote the business. You can't target parents if you're outside easy reach of residential property where families live. Similarly, if you want the commuter crowd you need to go to where the offices are, or where professionals live and will pass on their way to work.

Unless you know who you want your customers to be, and bring the product or service they want to them in a convenient way, you haven't got a hope. But once you do, it informs everything about how you operate and evolve the business. If you've got a commuting crowd coming in, can you sell them some breakfast on the go too? If your focus is freelance workers, can you get them to buy lunch as well as a few cups of coffee eked out over the working day? If it's mothers and toddlers, can you host meet-ups of National Childbirth Trust groups and similar? Without a detailed knowledge of who your customers are, all those opportunities are going to fly right past you.

What customers want isn't a secret. You can watch them, ask them and access research about them. You just have to look around you. How are customers in your industry behaving, what are they lacking and how can you create a service or product that bridges the two? It's not rocket science, but understanding your customer is the most fundamental building block of any business. Don't do anything until you're confident you know who your core customer is, what they want from you and how you can provide it, along with all the things they don't yet know they want.

Put yourself in the correct arena

In parallel with knowing your customers, you have to know your own business and the arena it is in. What I mean by that is understanding not just that you are a property business, or a shoe shop, but what kind. Every industry has a sliding scale – from premium to value, mainstream to boutique – and you have to know which label you wear and then act accordingly. If one day, Aldi started behaving like Marks & Spencer, and vice versa, you'd be left with a lot of confused customers, and far fewer sales. You don't go to Harrods to hunt for bargains, or to Bentley to buy a practical and cheap car!

Being in the correct arena matters, because it conditions how everyone from a customer to a potential investor approaches your business. Marketing your business is about creating expectations, and the service end is how you fulfil and ultimately exceed these. It all falls apart if you're not clear about what you're promising and don't follow through on the impression you have created in the mind of the customer.

It's also the case that people and companies become their environment: if you behave like a lower-league business then that's how you are going to be seen. If you want to be in the Premier League you have to act like it and go to the places and events that they do. Again, it's about picking an arena and working hard to establish yourself within it.

There's an element of self-fulfilment in this. You have to project the kind of business you want to be, which won't always match the reality on the ground to start with. With Asha's, the restaurant business I have owned with Pawan for the last decade, we acquired something that had been struggling under the ownership of Regents Inn Plc and where the management and staff wanted to take the business towards the cheap and cheerful marketplace. When I went in and said that we were going to raise menu prices, improve service and food standards and become a premium brand, the response was extremely negative. Most of the staff thought it would chase away any customers they already had.

But I was very clear about the arena I wanted that business to be in. I didn't want to be competing with the all-you-can-eat buffets or Balti Triangle curry houses. My vision was for a place where celebrities and people would want to come and be, to rub shoulders with the great and good and to celebrate birthdays and anniversaries. In other words, a premium offer with a sprinkling of stardust. The food is the best of its kind you can get in Birmingham, but what people really come for is the experience and the crowd, and they then become walking and talking ambassadors for our brand.

I wanted to create an award-winning, premium experience – one I was sure that customers would want as a special occasion destination. And that's exactly what we have created. Asha's is now fully recognized as a premium, award-winning restaurant brand that attracts celebrity diners, with an outstanding standard of food. In fact, as I write this section of the book, the Rolling Stones are busy celebrating Ronnie Wood's seventy-first birthday party at our Birmingham restaurant, following many other celebrities who have included Ed Sheeran, Chris De Burgh, sports stars and TV personalities.

That is an example of how to put a business in the correct arena, based on an understanding of what the customer wants, the potential of the business, and gaps in the market. You need to be confident about what arena you are placing your business in and then be consistent about the decisions you make to back up that aspiration and promise. Everything needs to reflect the brand and market reputation you are trying to build: no cheap crockery on the tables of an expensive restaurant, or 2-for-1 deals in a premium showroom. How you do anything must be how you do everything. Pick an arena, and stick to it.

Have a detailed and planned big picture, with ongoing strategies

Just as your life needs to have a big picture, so too does your business. Where do you want it to be in one, five and ten years' time? What is it going to look like in terms of scope, scale and diversification? All the same planning processes that I outlined in the previous chapter should apply. You need a big picture, backed up with goals, and they need to be detailed, challenging, realistic and desirable.

Beyond that, there are some specific points about the planning of a new business venture. The first is that you need a plan written down, though if it's a start-up this might be as simple as a few sides of A4. The plan should clearly express what the business is, who it's for and include all the relevant financial information and forecasts. There are templates and examples you can easily access online and through business advice services that show you the basics of what a business plan should include.

Once you've got the first draft of your plan, don't file it away in a drawer. Take it to someone with a bit of experience running a business in your industry. This is a crucial step, because for anyone starting out, there are going to be things you don't know, don't expect and won't have planned for. Someone who has been there before will be able to spot the pitfalls you haven't seen, sense-check your forecasts and give you a bit of a reality check about what is and isn't possible.

Don't think you know anyone who can perform this role? Then ask around. Almost anyone will know someone who knows someone, or you can simply reach out to people you are aware of and admire directly. You'd be surprised how well a properly pitched request for a bit of someone's time and advice may be received, however senior and eminent they may be. Look up the story of Reggie Nelson, a lad from London who at the age of seventeen went around the city's most affluent postcodes, knocking on people's doors and asking them how they had made their money. He chanced upon a senior executive from Blackrock, who went on to become his mentor, and a few years on he's a graduate with a good job in the City he could never have previously dreamt of.

Start with a detailed plan and, even if you have to go looking for one, find someone with some scars on their back to advise you on how to improve it.

You also need to make sure your plan has more than one string to its bow. It's not enough to say you want to do this one thing, and that will be the extent of your business. You also need ongoing strategies: new directions in which you plan to take the business over time, and ways in which you might feasibly diversify.

Let's return to the coffee shop example. There is a place in the village where I live, set up by a couple of young lads. I'm probably in there once or twice a week on average. It's always busy, but all they sell is coffee and cake. There's nothing for the health-conscious customer or for someone who wants to stop for lunch. I sit in there often thinking I'd like a sandwich, and then hear other people come in and ask the owners if they can do them a sandwich. I can almost guarantee that if they gave over their business to making sandwiches and coffee, they would double or even triple their turnover. The ongoing strategy for that business would be to diversify out of the elevenses and teatime business, and bring in a lunchtime crowd as well. In a small village, they would have something close to a captive market.

This is one example of a wider truth, which is that most businesses have untapped potential and capacity in them. There is usually more you could be doing to meet the needs of your customers: other services you could provide and different aspects of their activity or spend you can look to capture. Yes, doing more means more work, but if you are going to be working in that business so many hours a day anyway, why wouldn't you try to do the maximum possible in that time? No really successful business ever shirked an opportunity because it felt like too much like hard work.

A good business both understands the customer and has ongoing strategies to sell more to them over time, as a relationship is built. You can't expect to be successful if your business is a static entity, doing exactly the same as on Day 1, with no sense of evolution or change. Don't be stubborn about evolving your original idea, and be ready to swallow your pride. Your goal was a successful business that meets customer demand, not to fulfil a specific vision that is about to fall flat on its face. Be ready to adapt and diversify: your plan is a starting point, but it has to contain more than the first few steps you will take.

Have a fallback position, with a plan B or C in mind

Just as you need ongoing strategies, you must also have fallback positions prepared if your initial idea doesn't work out.

For start-ups, especially in fledgling fields, this is simply a natural part of how you evolve, as you work out what ideas are going to stick and which are destined to fail. Fallback positions are also about how well-established companies evolve, as technology and customer tastes change. Companies that succeed across generations only survive through their ability to adapt, as what was once their core business becomes less popular or even obsolete. In this way, Western Union – once a telegram provider – is now primarily focused on international money transfer. And IBM, world famous for its mainframes, is now reinventing itself as an artificial intelligence and cloud computing company.

Other famous firms haven't so much reinvented themselves, as reset a course they were already on. It's hard to imagine now, but Starbucks in its original form wouldn't sell you a cup of coffee. They retailed espresso machines and coffee beans for people to use at home. Only after the long-time CEO – then marketing director – Howard Schultz visited Italy and sampled its ubiquitous espresso bars did the focus change to creating shops where people could come to buy and drink a coffee. In this way, what had been a small chain of stores in the city of Seattle over time has become one of the world's most valuable brands.

Your business doesn't have to be an IBM or Starbucks to need fallback positions. Even if you are just opening that one coffee shop, you need the plan B or C to be in your mind – and written down – from the outset.

In my industry, this means you never acquire a property without having a very clear idea of what you would do in the case of an anchor tenant leaving, a market sector shifting unfavourably or some other unforeseen problem arising. We will never invest in something that doesn't have multiple routes to realizing value, whether that is through a change in use, demolishing the current building and starting from scratch or attracting a new kind of tenant. Beyond completely chance events like having your shop wiped out in a flood or hurricane (and even these things can depend on location and the likelihood of extreme weather – a reason you should buy insurance!), there shouldn't be much that happens to your business that is truly unexpected. Life may be full of surprises, but business shouldn't be. You need to anticipate the possible problems and plan your response, even if you hope it will never become necessary.

The importance of Plan B isn't just so you have something to fall back on. Often, the alternative will actually end up being a better route than the original plan. For years I have been buying up old 1970s office blocks, available at good prices because people can see which way that market is heading, as more people choose to work remotely or become self-employed. Plan A is to continue letting those offices as long as we can find tenants for them. But for those we can't, there is Plan B (alternative commercial use for hospitality, education or leisure) and Plan C (demolishing the offices and building houses in their place). Those secondary paths – especially the residential one – may well prove to be where the greatest value in those investments lies.

You need plans B and C not just in case of a problem emerging, but because they are often where the long-term opportunity lies in any business.

Continuously educate yourself and your business about the competition, changing markets and products

If I am going to invest in any new business, the first thing I will do is go out and look at what the competition is doing. You do not need to reinvent the wheel; in fact, you should be looking to learn, borrow and adopt as much as possible from those who have gone ahead of you. They are all finding out what customers do and don't want, and what is likely to work. There is always something you can learn from that.

One of the worst things you can be in business is insular. The shop or business you are running doesn't exist in a vacuum. It is part of a market of competitors, consumers and trends – and all are constantly changing. Unless you keep up with the pace of that change, ideally staying just ahead of it at all times, you are going to fall into irrelevance. If you don't get outside your business and see what is going on in your marketplace, all you'll learn about is what happens within your own four walls. That isn't the basis for building a business that evolves with the times, and crucially with the needs of its customers. A business that is insular will become static and unchanging, setting a limit on what it is able to achieve.

You get beyond the confines of your own company in two ways: reading about things and meeting people. Every industry will have its trade publications, journalists who write about it and analysts who commentate on it. Pick up the weekly trade mag and keep track of the writers and commentators. Don't let a major story in your sector pass by without knowing about it, understanding what it means and working out what you can do as a result.

I always tell the people who have just started working for me that they need to read the property press on both a daily (in national papers) and weekly (trade publications) basis. But the reading is only just the beginning. This isn't about flicking through the pages, glancing your eye across a few stories and feeling a bit better informed than you were before. The whole point of this exercise is that it tells you what is happening and provides a map towards new opportunities. In property, if you know who is buying or selling, you have an opportunity to put yourself in the middle. I can't emphasize enough how much I got done in the early days by just reading the *Estates Gazette* properly and following it up with a load of phone calls.

Some people act as if information is a precious secret, but the truth is that most of what you need to know is being printed on the pages and websites of publications that are accessible to all. In fact, now more than ever, the information you need as an investor or entrepreneur is available as the events themselves are happening. Keeping a close eye on it tells you about the people with buying power, new hires you should get to know and companies or markets that are in trouble. Most business opportunities arise from a change of one sort or another, whether that is something affecting the entire market or just one individual company. When fortunes fluctuate, yours can rise if you are abreast of the change and ready to take advantage.

You might expect me to say this since I'm writing a book, but one thing you often find with successful entrepreneurs and business people is that they read a lot. These are the busiest people, who you mightn't expect to have the time to immerse themselves in a book; but they make time because they appreciate the importance of learning. In the early stages of running a business you are learning by default, because so much is happening as you scramble to make it work, get hold of customers and then hold onto them. Over time, you have to work harder to keep learning, and that means putting the effort in. The ones who make it are those who never lose that appetite to learn new things and educate themselves about what is changing. It's the only way of making sure you don't get left behind by competitors and discarded by customers.

Learn to sell yourself – and your plan

At the early stage of setting up a business, a key skill is the ability to communicate your business plan and sell yourself. I'll talk next about the importance of networking, and this relies on developing the ability to succinctly and persuasively convey who you are and what you are doing. You can't shrug your shoulders and retreat into your shell when someone asks about your business. People will lose interest in someone who isn't confident and convincing about themselves and their plans.

For many, this is first tested around the launch phase when you are trying to raise funding for the business. Bank managers and venture capitalists have seen it all before. They are hard to impress and you have to be pitch perfect to convince them to part with their cash.

The very first fundraising we did for Bond Wolfe was to secure a £1,800 overdraft from our local bank. Twenty-five years later, as REI we went to the City and secured several investment rounds raising over £100m. Whatever the scale, the principles are basically the same: when you borrow from a bank, negotiate with a vendor or agent or recruit an adviser, you are selling yourself.

You need to be personally convincing and you need a plan (essentially a simple one) that demonstrates the money will be well spent and in all likelihood generate a handsome return. As any guide to pitching for funding will tell you, it's about the size of the addressable market, your unique ability to take advantage and the speed and size of the estimated yield.

A business plan is vitally important. But what people sometimes forget is that you aren't just selling investors a plan – you're also selling yourself as the person (or team) best equipped to deliver on it. When we got that tiny overdraft, it wasn't because we had some wonderfully innovative plan to upend the 1980s mortgage market. It was because a bank manager at NatWest called Ian Glaze made a judgement on Rory and me as people, decided he liked the look of us and knew we were putting everything we had into the business (emotionally and financially). It was the same pitching to institutional investors years later, when we showed how serious we were by putting in £10m of our own money.

Having sat on the other side of the table a few times now, I realize more than I did before that people are looking to invest in not just a good idea, but a person they can trust, and someone who has 'pain in the game'. At the moment we are working to expand the restaurant business I have mentioned. New venues are going to be led by the managers of our current restaurants. I know how good they are at the job, and because they are putting in a third of the funding, I also know that the level of their commitment is absolute. You're at your most confident as an investor when you know your money is going into something where the 'driver of the car' has a meaningful amount of their own money on the table, and will do everything in their power to succeed.

It doesn't matter whether you're raising small or large amounts, as a new or mature business – you have to get comfortable with your pitch, and above all with selling yourself.

The planning stage of any business is crucially important. If you set out without a detailed knowledge of the customer, or with a hazy sense of what arena your business is going to be in, and if you fail to have fallback plans and ongoing strategies for your business, it won't have the robustness and flexibility needed to survive inevitable bumps in the road.

Remember at the outset that you are not trying to build a cathedral in one go, but putting in solid foundations for a business that will only rise out of the ground with patience and application over the long term. You need those foundations to be broad enough to take the weight of everything that is to come.

If planning is what helps you to get a business in the right shape and arena, it is people that will help you grow it and make it a success. Next I will look at how you build a black book, cultivate a network and find a brilliant team of people to help turn your plan into a thriving business.

People

Cultivate relationships and build a network

The first thing to know about people in business is that it's useful to try to meet some. Yes, like it or not, you have to get out and network.

Networking is something a lot of people get anxious about, because working a room and introducing yourself to strangers doesn't come naturally to all of us. I was definitely in that camp at the beginning of my career. Compared to my business partner Rory, I was not gregarious or outgoing, and didn't look forward to attending networking events.

But whether you relish the prospect or not, networking is one of the fundamental business skills. It's every bit as important as being able to read a balance sheet or draft a lease. In some ways it's even more important, because while you can employ people to manage the various technical areas of your business, only you can represent yourself and build relationships. It's one of the few areas of business where there is no opportunity to delegate or outsource. It's you or nobody.

Like any other business skill, networking has its basic rules and you can learn how to get better at it. Learn how to look your best, introduce yourself to someone new and keep some conversation topics up your sleeve. Get comfortable with shaking hands, introducing mutual contacts and knowing how to finish a conversation as well as how to begin one. Remember that first impressions last, so consider your behaviour at these events and how that will be seen by others.

The unspoken truth is that most other people feel the same way about networking as you do. If you're feeling nervous, you won't be alone. If you're not a confident networker, find something you are confident about. In my case that was football, and I took that same mindset into corporate events, approaching it as I would have done a cup final. We all have something we know ourselves to be good at; you need to locate that well of confidence and use it in areas like networking where you are less sure of yourself. You put that cassette on in your head and just get on with the job.

There is no such thing as an inability to network, only a lack of confidence that can be addressed through coaching yourself in the basics and getting out there at every opportunity. And at the beginning, it *really* should be every opportunity. When you are trying to establish a business and a market reputation, you can't afford to miss out on any chance to meet people and pick up intel. You should be prepared to go to the opening of a bus stop, because you never know what you will hear or who you will meet. That breakfast meeting you had to drag yourself out of bed for could be the opening to a new deal opportunity, hire or meeting that proves transformative. Unless you go, you'll never know. Some invites will look like a waste of time, but there could be one person there who is your next important hire, investor or ambassador.

Remember also that you are building a network that will help underpin your career or business for decades. People you had forgotten about might pop up years later with an opportunity, because you once did them a favour or took the time to have a chat and introduce yourself properly. You never know when a relationship established at one point might bear fruit at another. This is also a way of creating good ambassadors for you and your brand. Today, with thirty-five years of network-building behind me, I can sit behind my desk and achieve most things I need with a couple of phone calls. But you need to work hard to get to that point: networking at breakfast, lunch and dinner. In years gone by, I would think nothing about starting the day early by dropping my gran off at the temple, attending an early meeting or event, doing a full day of work, picking gran up from the temple on the way home, coming home to see my family, and then putting on black tie and heading out again to attend a corporate dinner. It can feel like a hamster wheel, but the benefits of being diligent about networking are immeasurable.

I don't keep the same kind of schedule today that I once did, but even at this stage in my career I am still discovering the benefits of networking. In late 2014, for reasons that now escape me, I decided to get up early and attend a breakfast conference of the kind I would often now skip. There I met someone from something called the Business Growth Fund, an investment trust funded by the major banks to improve funding of growth companies. That initial conversation led to a meeting, when they told me about one of their portfolio companies, also in the property industry. Having got the inside track on them, it quickly became clear that they would be the perfect buyer for our auction business. And that's how we were able to sell that business, for many millions, without even putting it on the market. That would never have happened if I hadn't gone to that conference rather than giving myself an extra hour in bed.

One thing to remember about networking is that it doesn't begin and end at the event. A lot of people are happy just to have a chat, exchange business cards and get home to their family. But that's all a wasted effort unless you follow up with people you have met, who might prove to be mutually beneficial contacts. My golden rule is that a phone call either happens within twenty-four hours of the first meeting, or it won't happen at all. Act fast or you probably won't act at all.

As a more established business, you don't just attend networking events but often end up hosting them and promoting your business alongside local politicians and business figureheads. That's something we invest in, because it's always money well spent to bring the right people through your door and remind them what you are about. You don't stop networking once you've reached a certain stage; the process of meeting new people and adding to your contacts book should be a constant one at all stages of your career.

Ultimately, you need to network because you're not doing business with yourself. As a common Hindi phrase translates, you need two hands to clap. So go out and find a few to shake.

Surround yourself with a great team with whom you share the prize

'If you want to go fast, go alone; if you want to go far, go together.'

(African proverb)

I often say in my business that I don't do very much anymore. I'm only half joking: I have a brilliant team of people, some of whom have been working for me since the very beginning, and most of them are better at the different bits of running a business than I am.

Go and talk to any entrepreneur about how they built their company, and all of them will point to their team as the difference between success and failure. However good your ideas and instincts, you don't get very far without the right people around you to make things happen.

That means you have both to pick people well and, most importantly, you really need to look after them. I sometimes think about another property company in my area, which has done pretty well. But it loses staff members because when they ask for a pay rise, it doesn't happen. So they go off and have success elsewhere. And what could be a great business remains just a good one, because it can't hold onto enough of its people over the long term.

Retaining people starts with doing recruitment properly. It's not just about finding the people who you think could do the job brilliantly for a few years, but those who can fulfil their ambitions working within your business. I've turned down people in the past who would have been very successful hires in the short term, but whose focus was clearly on starting their own company before long. In that case you are better off staying in touch, keeping an eye on their progress and considering a different kind of relationship, like becoming an investor or partner.

For a successful hire, there needs to be alignment both on ambitions and values. You can't fundamentally disagree with the people you employ about the kind of business you are trying to build, or the way you do business. There is an important distinction here, because it's absolutely fine – and in fact, very helpful – to disagree about the means to a mutually agreed end. Seek out people who will challenge you, scrutinize your logic and stretch your thinking. But don't bring in those who want to set an entirely different direction, because that is always going to end in tears.

Because personal values are important, you need to look for more than technical skills and excellence when you are sourcing and interviewing candidates. If I sit down with someone, by the end of the interview I will have learned about more than their career history and professional successes. I'll know about their family, where they grew up and what their parents do for a living. You need to understand a person's environment to determine whether or not there is the scope for a good fit. You also have to be honest with people about what you are looking for. I always say to people that I hope to employ people who never want to leave, because they can achieve everything in their big picture working in my businesses. That is making sure you are aligned about each other's ambitions, and it's a crucial part of ensuring a lasting professional relationship. By the same token, if someone comes to you at the age of thirty having already had six or seven jobs, then they're never going to be a good hire for a company looking for loyalty and longevity.

As well as the individuals, you need to consider the timing of recruitment. Most companies are cyclical and know when they are going to be busiest in a given year or quarter. You should hire with this cycle in mind, but also seek to get ahead of it. Because if you bring people in just before the busiest period in the year, you've got a company full of staff who are still learning their jobs just at the moment when you need them operating at full speed. It's far better to recruit in advance, so by crunch time you have a battle-ready team in place.

Bringing the right people through the door is only half the job, if that. The most important thing is how you look after people: rewarding them, nurturing their careers and giving them the room to make progress in a way that's meaningful for them.

At the most basic level, that means being supportive where you can with pay and bonuses, giving equity to those who want to play at that level and ensuring that the cake is shared by all those who have helped to make it. Negotiating salaries and judging bonus levels is all part of good business and budgeting, so people don't always get what they want, but they must feel like they have a share in the success of the company and that their work is being rewarded beyond the base salary.

Looking after people is about more than pay and benefits. It also means understanding their lives – the highs and the lows – and doing what you can to support them in times of need. It takes nothing to send a text or make a call on someone's birthday, or to congratulate them on one of their kids graduating from university; and it's essential to understand when your employees are going through difficulties such as a bereavement or the breakdown of a long-term relationship.

As an employer you also need to have a clear sense of how you can help people progress with their careers. Sometimes you will see that their skills are developing in a certain area before they do, and they might be able to take on a role they hadn't previously considered. In other cases, it will be a matter of discussing with them a job they know they want to do and helping them plot a path towards it. You need to understand the big picture for your employees, and your role in helping them to fulfil it.

That involves giving them the support they need to progress, but also being honest and direct with criticism when it is needed. If someone says to you that they feel they are working too hard, but the reality is that they are turning up to work late at least one day a week, you are doing nobody any favours by not pointing that out. Similarly, if someone aspires to a certain position in the company, but does not yet behave and work in the way that the job would require, you need to make clear what you expect for that promotion to happen. (It's always the case that people should be acting as if they are already doing the next job, before you promote them into it.)

People make a business run, and as important as your outside network is, it's the ones you employ within a business who will ultimately make the difference between success and failure. Recruit carefully, be conscious of shared values and ambitions and be assiduous in how you reward people and coach them through their own careers. Reward people properly, and yours will be a loyal team that lasts the course and keeps your business on track.

Pick your professional advisers with care

You won't get far in business without having to seek professional help from lawyers, accountants or specialists in your particular field. You don't do even one property transaction without engaging a surveyor to complete a report and a lawyer to do the conveyancing.

This is a tricky area for entrepreneurs, because people in these fields are often very different from you and have different expectations about what represents good value. Many advisers expect to be paid for their time. A business owner will always expect to pay for results and nothing less. There is a cultural difference that can be hard to bridge. It's for this reason that you will often find successful people have something of a disdain for professional advisers and their pretensions.

But professional advisers are necessary, so you have to make a good job of picking them. My experience is that they come in two categories: the great and the totally fucking useless. The good ones are worth their weight in gold, and charge accordingly. You pay those fees because they reflect the quality of service you will receive. A good adviser is someone not just for a particular transaction, but who may well stick with you over years or even decades.

As your business evolves, you will need more and more specialist advisers, with experience of doing deals, budgeting and managing risk at different scales. But as you build this support team behind you, beware of the 'totally fucking useless' tendency in the professional world. These are the people who want to be you, on the client side making money, but don't have the instincts to make it happen. They like to think they know better than their client, when the truth is they couldn't recognize a real business opportunity if it bit them on the nose. Bad advisers are those who expect to be paid for turning up, and who will never tell you not to do a deal and thereby risk their fee.

The great ones see the bigger picture and know they will profit from establishing a productive relationship over the long term. And they recognize their role, which is to advise, not to act as if they are a player.

These advisers will make your business dealings more efficient, effective and profitable. But you need to choose with care.

Find the right partners

The wrong partner will destroy you and the right one will be the making of you. That applies as much to business partnerships as it does to marriages. Just as a spouse provides moral and emotional support, knows your mind sometimes better than you do, helps you make important decisions and tells you when you are making a mistake, a business partner is the essential counterbalance and co-pilot in the building of any serious company.

Your partner will most likely have different skills, a different personality and a different approach to doing business. As long as you are agreed on the overall direction, those differences are good things and not problems. Good companies are not autocratic in their approach and perspective, but benefit from a variety of different opinions and styles. That encourages the creative tension you need to weigh problems and opportunities from all angles before deciding what to do.

With most business partnerships there will also be an acceptance that you have contrasting strengths and perform different roles in the business accordingly. At the outset with Bond Wolfe, Rory was our front-of-house, sales and business development guy, while my focus was on strategy and deal-making. We also needed someone to run the finance side, but I probably didn't know anyone with a maths GCSE, let alone an accountancy qualification. 'My brother's an accountant,' I remember Rory saying. He was, and Marcus became the third pillar of a partnership that has lasted ever since.

As time has gone by, our skills and careers paths have evolved and diverged. Rory focused on the auctioneer role and wider auction business that became his specialism, while I progressed on investment, strategy and finance with Marcus, now REI's CFO. Like any relationship, if it is to survive, a commercial partnership needs to evolve as the needs and ambitions of those within it grow.

I tend to think that business partnerships need a skills mismatch (so you are covering all necessary bases), but a match on most other things: values, business ethics and big picture. You need the right range of skills, but most of all the right chemistry and a basic consensus about the appropriate way to do business. It's also important, especially at the early stages, to have parity of financial means and commitment. You don't want one person putting in considerably more capital than the others; there has to be parity for a partnership to work sustainably.

When you have a good partnership of equals and opposites, you need to stay with it and find ways to keep making it work as the context changes. Equally, a bad partnership can hold you back and you need to get out of it as soon as possible. A friend once walked away from a business in which he was the major stakeholder and which was doing extremely well. From the outside it looked like a bizarre decision, but he later told me that there had been one other shareholder – someone who only owned 1% but who still had a seat and a voice at the table – who was blocking his every move to try to evolve the business. So his only recourse was to get out, reinvest and start again in an environment where he wouldn't be held back by the wrong partner. Since leaving he has built a £1bn business, with full commitment to his own instincts and strategy and perhaps a point proved to the partners he left behind.

Above all, only enter into a partnership because you want to. It should never be out of necessity, or to try to access something the other person has, whether resources or relationships. It has to be because you like and respect the person and share a vision for the future with them. Partnerships forged out of expediency, rather than shared long-term ambition, are never going to make it far.

Most entrepreneurs will experience the ups and downs of business partnership if they are building companies for long enough. The successful ones have a knack for finding the right business partners, and separating themselves from the wrong ones.

Never deceive anybody and most of all never deceive yourself

Ever since my devout grandmother regularly took me to the local temple in Southall as a child, I have tried to live my life according to

Sikh values. Among the most important of these – one of the three pillars of the faith outlined by the founder of Sikhism, Guru Nanak – is *Kirat Karo*, which is about earning a living by honest and honourable means. You cannot deceive others in order to get ahead or create some sort of advantage for yourself through double-dealing.

That is a principle I have lived by in my career, and it is one that should be the philosophy of any entrepreneur. It's not just because this is the right thing to do, on a moral and social level. It's also the only way to build a sustainable business. If you go out seeking to deceive people in any way, it always catches up with you in the end. Doing business in this way means you are not building a proper company, but a house of cards that is always destined to collapse. However shiny and impressive it may look on the way up – and consider the plaudits that were once showered on Enron as an innovative company, or Bernie Madoff as an investment genius – a structure of this sort will always end up in pieces.

Those are the famous examples, but it's a lesson that applies on any scale. No one who has been deceived in even a small way by you will ever be a customer, an investor or a supporter again. More than that, they will tell all their friends and contacts, and you will lose more business as a result. You will be traducing your market reputation, one of the most important assets for any company.

Short cuts, by fair means or foul, simply do not exist in business or indeed in life. You need to do things the right, proper and honest way, earning a reputation for fair dealing and straight shooting. Build a reputation like that, and it will be your key bargaining chip in any negotiation. If people know what they are going to get, and trust your word, that can smooth over any number of other wrinkles on the way to securing a deal. You will then establish a reputation as a preferred buyer, investor, partner, employer and landlord.

Deceiving others is a major no-no for any business. Almost as bad, and probably a more widespread problem, are people who deceive themselves. This is when people convince themselves they are working as hard as they can, doing all the networking that time allows and doing everything in their power to share the cake with their staff. It's easy to justify stuff like this to yourself, but the reality on the ground will tell the true story.

Self-deception is a major barrier for many people in maximizing the success of their business and achieving their big picture. Most don't realize how much they are really capable of if they push themselves and set the bar that bit higher. If you are going to hit your goals and achieve your big picture, you need to learn how to get more out of yourself than initially seems possible. People who do that will surprise themselves with what they are able to accomplish. Others who convince themselves that they've done enough are just lying to themselves, and shouldn't be surprised when they fall short of expectations.

Never burn bridges or criticize companies, people or the competition

In any business, you will come across frustrations along the way. Partners will mess you around, contractors won't get the job done, and people will say one thing to your face and another behind your back. There will be many moments when you are tempted to let the market know exactly what you think of a certain individual or company. Don't do this. Resist the temptation every time, without exception.

Why? Because there's just no upside to it. It might feel good and vent some frustration, but it doesn't solve any problems or move you any further forward. In fact the only net effect is that you risk causing some kind of backlash or public slanging match as a result.

Whatever industry you are in will be a small world. Even a word in private with someone you think you can trust will get spread around and come back to you. Why would you do something that has the potential to create antagonism and damage your reputation? If you have the high ground after a deal of some sort has gone wrong, stay on it and keep your counsel.

Also remember that business is about the long term, and the person you encounter as a trainee might, before long, become an influential executive at a company you do regular business with. If you've given that person a hard time because they were junior, or shared your opinion that they didn't seem up to much, that can easily come back to bite you in the fullness of time. People have long memories, especially for personal slights. And people change. I've encountered some who I thought couldn't tie their own shoelaces, but they've improved over time and gone on to hold down serious jobs. Those people might change and evolve, but their impression of you will stay stuck in the moment when you disparaged them. So even if you think someone you've crossed paths with is a bit of an idiot, do yourself and them a favour and keep it to yourself.

Any business can be understood through the technicalities that underpin the products or services being sold. But no business succeeds on these things alone. When you have people as your customers, your counterparties and your partners, it is people who make the difference.

People decide whether or not a deal gets done, who gets the instruction and what your reputation in the market will be. An entrepreneur and their business will rise and fall based on the strength of their relationships – with the people they hire, the people they do business with and, ultimately, the customers they sell to.

That's why all of this networking, team-building and careful selection of partners and advisers matters so much. It is about investing in the right relationships that will make everything you want to achieve as a business possible. There are many obstacles a business can overcome, but having poor relationships is not one of them. So you have to invest in them: spend time, effort, money and energy on getting to know people and doing right by them. Always support and never bad-mouth. Be honest with yourself and those around you. Do all these things – nurturing a network, identifying talent and building a team – and your business will fulfil its potential.

With the planning and people behind you, it's time to focus on delivery, and how you get things done.

Delivery

Build, nurture and protect your most valuable asset: your market reputation

You've heard me mention market reputation a couple of times already, and this is an essential point to understand. Any business is a tangible entity made up of its assets, its employees and its trading performance. But it also exists as an idea and an expectation in people's heads. When someone thinks of REI, the first thing that comes to mind isn't the share price or the annual profit – it's what kind of a company we are to deal with, how we do business and what people say about working for us. This is the intangible asset of reputation: what others think of you.

Market reputation can be everything in business. It's what you trade off as much as capital and expertise. Don't mistake reputation for simply building a public profile and getting known. Publicity is one thing, but reputation is about being known for the right reasons. It's what produces repeat customers, recommendations and a sense of trust in your business.

Many of the things I've discussed here – putting yourself in the correct arena, never deceiving anyone, keeping critical opinions to yourself – are at their core about building a reputation for the kind of business you are and want to be. You achieve this through being consistent about delivering the best service, living up to your values and always doing exactly what you say you will. You want your business to be the byword in its industry for certain things, whether that is excellence, experience, expertise or value. These reputations are built by being rigorously consistent about how you work over time – a value brand like Primark can't just raise prices across the board if it's going through a tough patch, and a prestige company like Armani can't start selling from market stalls to reach more customers. Your brand is your market reputation, and everything you do has to fall in line behind it.

Market reputation can only be built over time – another example of why business and success are long-term pursuits – but it is an asset well worth the investment. Reputation doesn't just bring people to your door – it is what makes the difference in tight negotiations. If I'm talking to an agent who is trying to get a better price for their client, I will say that my offer isn't moving, but they know we don't mess around and the deal will go through without a problem. Because our reputation backs up that promise, we usually get the deals done at the price we want.

A reputation is the asset that money can't buy. It can only be earned through consistent investment in doing the right thing and building a business that is as good as its word. You have to be relentless about building your market reputation and use it as a lens to consider every hire, every deal and every partnership you enter into. Does the thing you're about to do add or detract from it? Never do anything that risks undermining your reputation, even if it seems like easy money to do so. Remember there is an intrinsic value to reputation that can't be seen on the balance sheet, but nevertheless helps you over time to grow profitability and value. If you are mindful of your reputation, invest in it and safeguard it at all times; it will pay a long-term dividend for your business.

Think until it hurts, to outsmart the competition

'Poor thinkers will never be rich.'

PAUL BASSI CBE

Business is a contact sport, and there is no industry where you get the luxury of operating without competitors. But although you can't get rid of your competitors, you can get away from them. The aim should always be to operate in a market of one or few, while the majority are chasing the more obvious opportunities and getting in each other's way.

Whether you are dealing with a problem or trying to seek new avenues, there will always be an obvious way to go. But you shouldn't go there, because you can guarantee that most of the market will also be rushing headlong in that direction. Remember the danger of the bandwagon?

Instead, as I often say to our team, you need to think until it hurts. Find another angle on the market you are in, look for where the under-served customers are or the under-invested segment lies. Most markets appear busy, but that is because the attention of investors and commentators is on where the activity is. No one talks about the untapped opportunities until someone has started to make waves, and at that point another bandwagon will start rolling, hopefully well behind you. It's just as they say: a poor thinker will never be rich.

We did this with Asha's, driving it as I described towards the premium end of the market, while the apparent gold rush ten years ago was towards all-you-can-eat buffets. Many of those have closed now, because like any market that overheats, you get too many entrants and a good number are doomed to fail.

In my property career, I have always looked for assets that others think are in distress – whether old office blocks or high street retail – knowing that there is an opportunity to be realized through a combination of effective management and a long-term approach.

Most people in business only touch the surface of the markets they are operating in. They reach for the first solution that presents itself, which will always be the most obvious and as a result the most heavily competed for. They throw themselves into the toughest sector of the market, where competition is fiercest and value is hardest to find.

If you take that road, you are operating at the highest level of difficulty, making the challenging job of building a successful business even more challenging than it needs to be. Instead, think harder, separate yourself from the noise of what everyone tells you is the only solution, and work on some alternatives. Go where the market isn't and you will often find that's where the opportunity lies.

When you have a proven strategy, fire a torpedo not a bullet

As you do that hard thinking, you will bring to the surface all sorts of possible avenues for your business. Most companies have the potential to diversify in them. If you are doing one thing for customers that gets them through the door, it's simple commercial instinct to seek other products and services you can provide. That's why what I started as a brokerage business successively branched out into estate agency, property investment and management, auctions and now bridging finance and hospitality. There is always more you can do for the customer and to build the scope and scale of your business.

It's not just about the ability to recognize these opportunities, but what you make of them. A lot of people are content to do what I call firing bullets at the opportunity: doing a few things but not really committing to drive the business in a new direction. They want the upside without taking the risks that can unlock serious returns. By contrast, the most successful companies will see an opportunity and, having fired a few bullets to scope its potential, fire a torpedo at it. They are willing to rewrite their business model, redirect focus and investment and pursue the new direction at full throttle.

A good example is Whitbread, which began life as a brewing company and has in more recent times had major investments in the restaurant and fitness industries. At the time of writing, it has just parted with Costa Coffee and is preparing to fire a torpedo at the budget hotel business, opening a new 'no frills' chain that will sit alongside its core holding, Premier Inn.

Moves like this are never done lightly, nor should they be. Note that I am advising to fire your torpedo at a proven strategy, not one whose potential you have just started to glimpse. You might well want to cast a few bullets in a few different directions to determine where the most relevant opportunity for your business lies. Experimenting in this way is an important part of learning and gathering necessary intelligence. There might be hidden hurdles you hadn't foreseen, or the opportunity may not be what you had assumed it to be. These need to be explored to avoid making a costly and commercially fatal error when you launch the torpedo.

But you cannot spread your bets forever if you are going to maximize your company's potential. There is always a time to decide and work out where to focus your maximum talent, capital and energy. Often that will mean getting out of a market that has delivered for you in the past, to free up all of the above. The most successful companies make that decision and act accordingly, where others that do ok never quite pluck up the courage to load up a torpedo.

How you attack new commercial opportunities, and the extent to which you are prepared to put your money where your mouth is, will be among the key factors that determines how successful your business will become. It's at these moments that you have to decide whether you are willing to dive in at the deep end, or are content to remain paddling around with the certainty of the ground beneath you. Real success demands that you throw everything you have at the best opportunity you have found in the market. You need to be ready to fire that torpedo when the moment comes.

'Secret' cost-free projects to identify new markets and opportunities

As you are working out where and how to fire your torpedo, you need to prepare your business for the change that likely lies ahead. In order to avoid firing blind, you need to experiment in the areas you believe to hold the biggest potential.

Aim to do this cost free. Don't build an expensive, all-singing-and-dancing machine to test out your hunch. Instead, beg and borrow time and resources that are already costed in the business to run an experiment. Carve out a proportion of some people's time to work on the new business area, without taking them off their full-time jobs. Then, as the new idea develops, appoint an individual or team to further investigate the opportunity and market-test it. At all times keep yourself engaged and only when you have a clear proposition in place, one that has been costed and tested, should you make the decision to fire your torpedo.

We have done this recently in the area of bridging finance. We know the customers exist, we can provide what they want (a certainty they increasingly struggle to get from banks) and it fits well with our other businesses, particularly the property auction house.

But we haven't gone into this market without reconnaissance, convinced though we are of the opportunity. Instead, we ran a two-year test drive, with a couple of the existing team dedicating some of their time towards building the structure of a lending business and starting to write loans. Now we are ready to launch the business, it has basically cost us nothing and we already have a system and operation up and running, one I have kept a close eye on and have full faith in. It's at this point that I will look to hire people specifically to run that side of the business. And we will grow it as a fully costed, budgeted concern, with the same rigorous forecasting and targets as the rest of the company.

Had we taken the opposite approach and sought to build the finance business as a going concern from Day 1, investing in a separate team and P&L, it would have been a significant investment just to get the operation to the stage it has now reached with no meaningful investment at all, and could have been a project that we ended up aborting after further investigation and significant cost.

When you have identified an opportune market to expand and diversify into, you will, as I have described, eventually want to fire a torpedo of capital and talent at it. Seizing the opportunity will be an expensive and labour-intensive operation. But exploring it shouldn't be. Work cost-free until you have reached the point where you need to invest heavyweight capital and resources.

Avoid winning battles at the expense of winning wars

Everything that you are doing to build your business is ultimately a part of how you achieve your big picture. But beware, because the road from here to there is full of bumps, potholes and dangerous drivers, all of which threaten to take you off course. In any given week, challenges will present themselves, whether that is a problem with an employee, a deal that is hitting the buffers, a change in legislation, a political or economic event or an unforeseen issue somewhere in your business (with a tenant, a client, or some aspect of your supply chain or production line if you are in those industries).

Some of these are problems that need to be solved, and you must divert your focus to avoid being left with an even bigger issue. But many are not. Many of the challenges that cross your desk and crop up in your personal life will simply not be worth the trouble. Some don't have straightforward solutions, others aren't as important as they initially seem and still more are simply distractions masquerading as serious problems.

Successful entrepreneurs are compulsive about winning, but they also understand the benefit of a tactical retreat that serves the big picture. If a deal that you really wanted to do is running into difficulties, don't keep investing time and effort in it. Let it go and find another one. If something you are trying to make happen won't – in our case if we can't get a property sold – then switch focus to other things you can achieve. Give attention to the things you are able to do and the areas where you can make a difference. If you run up against a brick wall, accept the setback and don't get hung up on trying to blast your way through. There will be another, more efficient and profitable way around, quite often better than the initial opportunity you identified.

Problems loom large in the collective mind of any business. But if you start throwing people and capital at them, you will often end up achieving nothing, and actively harm other parts of your business that get temporarily forgotten as you all focus efforts on this one issue.

It's important to keep a sense of perspective when you run into what look like difficulties. What in one moment feels like a major issue will, from the standpoint of a few months and several deals later, seem insignificant. That property that wouldn't sell will eventually find a buyer, and by the time it has, it won't seem like the big problem you once thought it was.

You need to learn the difference between a serious problem that needs to be nipped in the bud, and a distraction that will cost more than it earns to take seriously. On the road to your big picture, you aren't going to get very far if you spend the whole time filling in potholes.

The same point applies when it comes down to specific deals or negotiations. In a recent episode, an investment that was worth millions was being held up on the basis of a £40,000 cost, the responsibility for which was disputed. The whole thing could have collapsed on the basis of that alone, but I spoke to the counterparty, and we agreed that the disputed money should be placed in escrow and that the question would be sorted out after the deal had been completed. Meanwhile the deal went through, because we focused on achieving the ultimate objective, not letting one small problem derail the whole process. It's always worth losing a battle if it clears out an obstacle that makes it easier to win the war. Don't let your pride get in the way of accepting a loss or compromise that serves your greater commercial good.

Work on your business, not in it

As the founder or CEO of a business, you need to accept that your role is going to change over time. In fact your goal should be to make yourself redundant from almost every role, because you have found someone brilliant to fill it on your behalf.

At the very outset, you will often do multiple jobs because there is no one else to do them. You're the company's sales rep, financial controller and marketing guru all at the same time. Like the box-to-box midfielder in a football team, you are covering every inch of ground possible to stay ahead in the game. Then, as you grow and recruit, others start to do much of that running for you. Eventually you're not a player at all, but a manager on the touchline, deciding the tactics and sending the team out to play. Then you're up in the stands and the corporate box, observing from on high.

If you are going to keep running the business as it changes, these are evolutions you need to get comfortable with. Just as player-managers have rarely been successful in elite football, a good chief executive doesn't try to put themselves on the pitch at the same time as managing the team and chairing the board. There isn't time to do all of those jobs well, and one or all of them will suffer. Plus, remember you recruited a team to play for you, and you need to let them do that.

It's for these reasons that I often think the best entrepreneurs are 'on' their businesses, not 'in' them. Like the manager or club owner sitting in the stands, they are watching the same game as the players, but they have a different perspective and role. Their job is to see the big picture, from higher up, which is very different from how things look in the rough and tumble on the pitch. When I started out, I was the guy who went out and valued properties for clients; but I probably haven't done that now for thirty years. You have to move on to make progress and clear the path for young talent to mature.

The company leaders who stumble and fall are those who spend too much time 'in' their businesses, dealing with the everyday ups and downs that are better left to the people you hired for exactly those jobs. As a result, these leaders don't spend enough time focusing on relationship-building, identifying new opportunities and fulfilling their role as public ambassadors for their firms. They secretly hanker for the days when they were on the pitch playing, and don't want to accept the necessity of a change in role, or don't quite have the trust in their team needed to delegate. For those people, the only answer is to relinquish an executive role, because the truth is they don't really want to do it. That's fine, but it's important to be clear about it: another example of why being honest with yourself is so important. Some leaders simply don't have the skill set or confidence to move forward.

If you do want to keep on running your business, then get used to taking a step back, letting people get on with the jobs you hired them to do, and accepting that your input isn't always necessary (or indeed helpful). Be disciplined about sticking to your job, which is to see the big picture and do what is necessary to move the business towards it – whether that is through good hiring, exploring new opportunities to diversify or establishing strategic partnerships.

That is not to say that you should never get involved in the day-to-day running of your own company. But remember that your interventions carry weight and must be carefully judged to ease difficult situations and not compound them. An idle comment or suggestion from the boss can easily send a team haring off in the wrong direction, as they rush to put your idea to work and cast aside more important tasks. But there are times where you can help and make a difference, leveraging your reputation and relationships to help your team do their job. Often I will assist with the closing of deals, where a phone call from me can speed up the process or help remove a roadblock. That can sometimes achieve in a few minutes what would otherwise have taken days or weeks. In addition, a counterparty often appreciates the respect that is conveyed by the chief executive picking up the phone to negotiate.

It's also worth noting that you can't be 'on' a business if you've never actually been in it. Knowing your business from the ground up and understanding the jobs of everyone who works for you (probably because you once did them yourself) is essential. That equips you to know when someone is missing a trick, overstating a problem or overlooking a risk. A friend of mine, Ranjit Boparan (aka the Chicken King), founded what has become one of the UK's largest food businesses, employing over 23,000 people and supplying chicken to all the major retailers. Going to meet him one time to discuss a joint venture, he greeted me but was unable to shake my hand because his were covered in chicken fat and blood, having just come from the production line. He had started on the factory floor at the age of sixteen and ensured he never lost that perspective even as he built a business that turns over billions every year. You have to stay on the business, but you also need a willingness to get your hands dirty. Keeping your hand in is important, even if that means getting it messy.

Running a company that is well established, as opposed to a start-up in its earliest stages, requires considerable discipline on the part of the individual at the top of the tree. You can't give in to the temptation to micro-manage people who are good at their job and know it inside out (probably better than you). Instead you have to judge when and how to weigh in, but most importantly when to get out of the way. Remember what your role is and stick to it.

Specialize and stick to your knitting

Do what you know. 'Stick to your knitting.' You might have heard these words said before in an almost derogatory sense, when people are told to know their place. But it is also very sensible business advice.

Those who succeed in business do so because they get to know an area very well. They develop deep wells of market intelligence, a huge network of contacts and an intuitive sense – one acquired through experience – of what does and doesn't represent good value. Every decision they make and every deal they do is stronger because of what they know, who they know and what they are known for (their market reputation). You become better informed and better able to prosper in your chosen field as the result of an accumulation of all of these things. Market intelligence, contacts, experience and capital all grow and mutually reinforce each other over time.

Step too far away from that arena, and suddenly those advantages start to slip away. People don't know who you are anymore, or what they can expect. Even worse, you don't have the same insight or confidence. It's for this reason that a lot of well-established brands in one country will fall on their faces when they try to repeat the trick overseas. Tesco famously stumbled with its US brand – Fresh and Easy – which confused American consumers about what it was meant to be (and could trade off none of the immediate association with value that the Tesco brand has built in its home market). It never made a profit in seven years of trading. More recently Wesfarmers, one of Australia's

biggest companies, lost hundreds of millions by writing down its
acquisition of the DIY chain Homebase. It had attempted to replicate
the Bunnings Warehouse model popular down under, but alienated
consumers by cutting promotional deals and confused them with car
park barbeques that made little sense in the UK context and climate.
Having acquired the business amid hot competition for £340m, it
ended up having to sell it for £1 just two years later.

Those examples go to show how even the mighty and handsomely
capitalized can fall when they venture too far from the markets and
sectors which they know and in which they are well known. My own,
less dramatic but still challenging, example of the same was when I
took guidance from a financial adviser to diversify some investment
out of property into a foreign exchange vehicle. This was a disaster
that left me swallowing a seven-figure loss, even after compensation
for bad advice. Remember, an adviser will never take responsibility for
their mistakes!

What that taught me – and a mistake is only a mistake if you don't
learn something from it – is that I should stick to investing my own
money and put it into what I know. That's why I have stuck consistently
with Midlands property throughout my career. We know how to find
good deals, our network within that village is about as good as it could
be, and after over thirty-five years our market reputation does a lot of
the heavy lifting for us. Sticking to my knitting – from both a sector
and a geographical perspective – has been fundamental. It is playing
on home turf, where you know the territory and have the key assets of
knowledge and reputation in your favour.

This isn't to say you can't diversify. Just as my property business has
over time grown to encompass everything from writing mortgages

and estate agency to investing in properties, managing, selling and auctioning them, and providing bridging finance, you can expand the scope of what you are doing.

In the early days, people would tell me that I was making a mistake by not specializing in either the estate agency, the mortgage brokering or the investing. But I didn't see why that had to be the case, and although I increasingly focused on the investment side over time, having the agency business – and later the auction house – was a critical part of how we informed that side of the business. We'd never have made nearly as much money by just being agents or auctioneers, and by the same token we would have been much less effective investors without the constant flow of live market intelligence that those other businesses provided, being as close to the customer as they are by nature. The spreadsheet doesn't always tell you the value of a business like that, if it is making a significant, intangible contribution to the success of another part of your overall mix.

Stay rooted in the realm of what you know: the industry, the geography, the culture. If you get too far beyond what you know, then all the advantages you have in your primary field start to fall away. And then you are beyond taking calculated, well-informed risks, and into the area of the outright gamble. By all means expand your canvas and the different threads in it over time, but remember to stick to your knitting and not venture too far into unfamiliar territory.

Avoid burnout

It's undoubtedly true that you need to be relentless to build a successful business. But there are also limits to how hard any one person can work. So while you charge towards your big picture and pack as much as possible into every day, you also need to be mindful of the threat of burnout.

This was brought home to me one day in my late forties, when I very quickly went from feeling a bit ropey to having a doctor send an ambulance for me and undergoing an emergency heart operation. My arteries were blocking up, and if I hadn't gone into hospital that day, the worst could have happened.

Bear in mind I don't smoke or drink, and I've always kept myself in reasonably good shape. But overwork carries its own dangers, regardless of how cleanly you live in other areas of life.

This was around the peak of the financial crisis, when we were in the early days of building the REI portfolio. I had business stresses, some family concerns and other commitments that made very little of my time my own. Mentally, I was able to take the strain, but without warning my body had started to buckle.

The dangers of overwork are well documented. People who on average work longer hours, especially in sedentary roles, are more susceptible to everything from heart disease to strokes and premature death.

So how can you square the circle between putting in the hours needed to make your business a success and ensuring you don't fall into the burnout trap? The most important thing is knowing how to look after yourself, and being clear about what your limits are. We all know when we have reached that point when we need a break, and it would be fruitless to carry on working. You have to listen to that voice and do whatever helps you to relax: whether that's a day with your family at home, getting yourself to the gym or shutting yourself off from business communications for a weekend. You can be relentless about your work and still know when to take a break and recharge.

It's also useful to find routines that help you to relax and get into a positive frame of mind. A couple of times a week, I will use a technique I adapted from the author Hal Elrod and his book *The Miracle Morning*. It involves getting up half an hour earlier than usual and going through the following steps:

Senses: A few moments of meditation. Slowing down your pulse, listening to yourself breathe, and gathering your senses.

Affirmations: Repeat the goals that you are working on at the moment. I will do that deal. I will solve that problem. Affirm what you are focusing on and your ability to achieve it.

Visualizations: After affirming my goals, I then try to visualize what achieving them will look like. If I'm trying to sell a property, I'll imagine the lawyer calling me up to confirm the deal has gone through.

Exercise: Wake yourself up with a bit of exercise, even something light like yoga or stretching.

Read or write: Take twenty minutes to have a read of your book, or something you wouldn't normally have time for. Or do a bit of writing you've been putting off . . . a letter to a friend.

Spiritual: At this point I say a short prayer.

Gratitude: Finish up the routine by remembering what you have to be thankful for: good health, a wonderful family, a business to run.

This is half an hour out of my morning, one that sets me up for the rest of the day and everything I will go on to do over the hours that follow. I see it as one of the most important things I do to maintain equilibrium and focus my mind.

My other routines are the gym three times a week and going to the temple once. These are small things, but all part of making sure I am in the best physical and mental shape to give my all to work and family. It's simple: as Robin Sharma has noted, **'If you don't make time for exercise, you'll probably have to make time for illness.'** It always catches up with you in the end.

A business might fill most of your waking hours, but carving out time to do things that calm you down and offer perspective is an essential part of any busy week. Make sure, as much as you are charging towards that next deal or target, that you are also looking after yourself and keeping the spectre of burnout at bay.

Do not quit

However you manage your time and build in the opportunity to rest and relax, you also need to remember one final thing. Do not quit.

The reality is that most people quit. It's just in them to give up when the challenge becomes too great or the slog too hard. Another tough negotiation, another problem to deal with, another year where you don't spend enough time with your kids just feels like too much. Especially for those who have already made enough to be comfortable, the beach often beckons.

If you want to fulfil your big picture, this is not an option. You don't achieve ambitions like this by leaving a job half done. A really successful business isn't one that you build and run well for a few years, even a decade or two: it's something lasting that will continue to grow after you have gone, a legacy for the next generation. Whatever you are feeling in the moment, you will always regret not having buckled down and carried on.

There were many times where I could have given up, decided I had come far enough and had achieved more than most ever expected of me. But I don't have it in me to quit. I know I can only fulfil my big picture if I keep going, come what may.

The importance of never quitting applies to your core business and big picture. In the course of pursuing those, you may have to give up on other interests that end up being conflicts or which drain your time. I benefited in many ways from my involvement in groups like the Chamber of Commerce. But a few years ago, I had got myself into a situation where I had a number of non-executive directorships running in parallel. Meetings and obligations that weren't fundamental to my big picture were piling up. I remember walking around Birmingham one summer afternoon in a bit of a daze, realizing that I had overcommitted myself and needed to create more time and space for the core business. So I took the decision to give up my outside interests. I didn't just write letters and run: I went and met every organization to explain the reason why. It wasn't necessarily something I wanted to do, but it was the right decision at that point.

So yes, there is a time to quit – but never on yourself, your business or your big picture. Kaizen, the art of continued progress and purpose, is for you, your health and your mental wellbeing. Those who practise Kaizen usually live longer, healthier and more fulfilled lives.

6

Learning how to make, save and spend money

A wise person should have money in their head,
but not in their heart.

JONATHAN SWIFT

As I have said, money is not anyone's big picture. And it is not the end goal of any business either. But to achieve those goals and fulfil that big picture, you will still need to learn how to make money through your business. To manage money effectively, you need to know not just how to make it, but also how to save and spend. Here are my top tips.

Making money

It's all about income, income, income. Create multiple income streams from rent, trading, dividends and profit; and build up cash for reinvestment and to cover your lifestyle and overheads.

Capital gains and windfalls are very welcome but should not be relied upon, as they are infrequent. When you do have one, reinvest it to generate more income, funding a virtuous cycle of increased income and, over time, greater dividends.

Make sure you have good accountancy and tax advice, so that you constantly provide for your tax liabilities and maximize your tax allowances.

Saving money

Think about saving as a process of building up capital to reinvest and create new income streams. Obviously, you need enough to cover your overheads and lifestyle. Do not live beyond your means, as some entrepreneurs do, and always make sure you have a cash reserve so you don't feel financially pressured.

Build up cash reserves and reinvest. Start by saving 10% of your income. As you become more successful, this is a level you should be able to comfortably live off.

By saving, you put yourself in a position to capitalize on great opportunities and market downturns whenever they may arise. In property you will build up a portfolio of bricks and mortar, but you need liquid assets too so you can access capital quickly when the time is right.

Spending money

Enjoy your income, and invest in assets rather than racking up liabilities. Understand the difference between an income-generating asset and a depreciating one. With the latter, think about renting them, and only buy if the loss in value isn't going to matter to you.

Use 10% of your windfalls to treat yourself and those around you, then reinvest the balance. Enjoy it with family and friends, have amazing experiences and create memories. Otherwise what has all the relentless hard work been for?

Use your resources for good

When it comes to spending your winnings, you need to think about how you are going to share the cake. I've already discussed why this matters in the context of building a loyal team of people around you. But you shouldn't just share within the four walls of your company. The most meaningful thing isn't making the money, it's what you then go on to do with it. That means you need to make a contribution to your community, giving money to worthy causes and changing other people's lives for the better.

As Bill Gates said, **'with great wealth comes great responsibility'**. I certainly don't have great wealth, but the principle is an important one for anyone who has made more money than they need to support themselves and their family. The Scottish philanthropist Andrew Carnegie understood the same. He said that **'the man who dies . . . rich, dies disgraced'**.

My belief in this is rooted in another of the three pillars of Sikhism, *Vaṇḍ Chhakō* – sharing what you have with the community. In Sikh temples, visitors who need or want to be fed will always get a free meal, funded by the local community.

I believe the same should apply in business. For years, our Bond Wolfe Charitable Trust has been raising money and making donations to local charities, working in areas such as supporting children with cancer in finding treatment and funding women's refuges. As I've mentioned, I am especially proud of Sandwell Valley School, which we were instrumental in helping to establish.

Money is important, and every successful company should find ways to use its wealth to support community interests. But it's not just about cash donations here and there. I like to think in terms of what I call 'resource': all the assets and tools at the disposal of a company. This is about more than money: it's your network and ability to convene, your reputation, the skills in your business, your ability to influence the public debate. Resource is your whole commercial toolbox, and you need to open it up to the benefit of your local community.

For example, I was recently approached by an organization that works to tackle the skills gap in big cities, addressing the fact that places like Birmingham have fast economic growth but a low skills base, and too many young people who lack the education and skills to take on the jobs now being created. The organization needed investment to roll out a programme that had been successfully piloted elsewhere. I could have put a bit of money in the pot and left it at that. But there was a more useful deployment of our resource: bringing together a roundtable of over a dozen property industry players, some with deeper pockets than ours, and getting them all focused on the need and the issue. That has provided the charity in question with a short cut to multiple sources of funding: it was the best and most efficient use of our resource to help achieve some good.

The ways in which a business can leverage their resource for community benefit vary significantly. It can be about donating space or the time of your staff, or acting as a convenor. It can be helping a charity bang the drum for its project and raise far more money than you could provide as a donor in isolation. The connectivity that you need to build up your business has more uses than just making money. Every business should find ways to use their connectivity for the wider good. There is really no point doing well unless you are also prepared to do some good.

7

Successful property investing

Do what is right, not what is easy, nor what is popular.
ROY T. BENNETT

It's a long-established fact that the UK loves to invest in property. Almost two-thirds of the population own the home in which they live. As of 2018, there are a record 2.5 million buy-to-let landlords. Investors enjoy the tangible security and generally steady returns that a solid property asset can deliver. For first-generation immigrants, property has often been the route from nothing to something. It meant my dad, who arrived in the country with £2 in his pocket, ended up doing a deal worth three-quarters of a million.

But although the UK property market is full of punters, you can't afford to approach it in an amateurish way. Good property investing isn't a particularly complex business, but it is one that requires an informed and disciplined approach. You need to have rock-solid market intelligence, a strong network of relationships and crucially you have to buy well. You need to know what the right price is, how much debt to take on, how you add value to an investment, the mechanics of management and the risks inherent in any property holding. Most people don't know these things: they just buy, ride the market cycle and hope to get lucky. By doing so they fail to make the most of their investments in a good market and get burned in a bad one. Property is not a complex or heavily regulated business – you don't need to get a professional qualification to invest as you would to become a plasterer or electrician. But as fundamentally simple as it may be, it does have some essential disciplines and laws that you need to grasp before putting any money down.

The same principles apply whether you are an investment group with a portfolio running into the billions or getting ready to buy your first investment property. These are the fundamentals I have learned from buying my first houses in the 1980s through to investing directly in property worth hundreds of millions, and working alongside and observing other investors whose portfolios are considerably larger. A good investment doesn't have to be a massive play, but it does have to be done right. This is how you can do that. Again, I've divided my advice into sections:

Market intelligence and relationships: everything you need to do before putting money on the table – developing knowledge and market intelligence, building the right relationships and finding good advisers.

Buying well and making a profit: how to strike good deals and go from a good entry price to a great return, as a proactive investor who adds value and manages risk.

Market intelligence and relationships

It's not location, location, location – it's market intelligence

Location is usually the first thing that comes to mind when people think about property. It's the Monopoly board philosophy: land on the right square and you will be guaranteed a good return. Except location isn't the real fundamental that determines the worth of a property investment: as I'll explain, that is your entry price. The idea that there are good locations and bad ones is too simplistic. The reality is there are smart deals to be had everywhere, and ones to be avoided. I have spent my whole career investing in property around the West Bromwich and Birmingham areas. It's only in the last couple of years that the West Midlands has started to be seen as an attractive investment destination, a far cry from where we were in the 1980s. But there were good deals then as there are now – if you knew where to look.

This latter point is the key, which is why I tell people to think first not about location, but market intelligence. Remember that the value of any given location is not fixed, but constantly changing. You might have a run-down, scrubby piece of land on the edge of a town centre that can't be sold for love nor money. But if a McDonalds drive thru is about to open there, that is suddenly going to become a prime development and investment spot. In that case, the value of the location changes overnight, but it's only by having the market intelligence before the rest that you can take advantage. Of course location matters: but the worth and potential of a place are fluid entities, determined by what you know to be changing – your market intelligence.

Everything you need to make a successful property deal – knowing the right entry price, the headroom for capital growth, the gearing, the risks to be priced in – is dependent on your market intelligence. You need an insight into both what an area is like right now and the factors that will be driving change – new investments or developments – to get all of those critical judgements right. And in the case of an individual property, you need to know the circumstances of the vendor: a prosperous property fund in a growing economy is unlikely to sell to you for a good price; but one that has gone into receivership and has a bank looking to realize the asset quickly will give you a very good deal. Market intelligence tells you when, how and from whom you should be looking to buy. It's about knowing what the present and future of a specific building or area looks like, and in a negotiation, being able to see as many of the cards your counterparty is holding as possible.

You should never go into any property investment without knowing your day 1 profit (immediate earnings) and your projected return: the baseline expectation for what that the asset is going to deliver once you have made your improvements, ridden the property cycle and sold it well. That might go up if conditions favour you, but it should be calculated in a realistic enough way that it never goes down, barring a total disaster of some sort. You don't invest on a whim or a hope that things might turn out well for you. It all has to be mapped out in your head: what you are going to do with it and how that will realize value and deliver a profit.

That calculation is only possible if you have your market intelligence lined up. You need to know everything about the area and type of property you are investing in, and any customers (tenants) involved. You need to know these things as they apply right now and to understand how they are likely to evolve over the course of your investment. Very little happens in this market that is unforeseeable if you have thought about it hard enough. There are always early signs of the changes that are going to affect the value of an investment – whether it's shifts in overall economic conditions, the specific life cycle of tenants, or new developments coming onstream. There shouldn't be accidents or surprises along the way. You need to get your market intelligence lined up before you even think about putting money on the table.

How is this done? There are three ways: getting to know your patch, educating yourself about the market and forming good agent relationships.

Know your patch

Never invest in a place until you really know it. It's not enough to pore over data tables of house price growth, or to look at postcodes where rents still have the most scope to be increased (although you absolutely need to know this information and to have an intuitive sense for what market value looks like in a given area). You need the evidence of your own eyes as well. To understand an area, and to get to know your patch, it's not enough to browse Rightmove occasionally, dip into the local press or make occasional visits. You have to be in the area, knowing the place, its people and its rhythms.

Let me explain. I like to buy high street retail, and have done for the whole of my career. But I don't know if something will be worth the investment until I take the time to go and survey it myself. I need to see the kind of people who are shopping there: the clothes they're wearing and the cars they're buying. Just as any proper business owner knows their customer, as a property investor you need to know the customer's customer, the end user. Don't buy the freehold for a parade of shops until you have as good a sense of the customer as you would need to run that business yourself. Invest the time in understanding the supply and demand, the flows of people and the untapped opportunities. What's the mix of residents and visitors? Are the shops and cafes as busy as you would expect? Is there scope for the sort of refurbishment and upgrade that could mean rent increases? Which shops are on the busy side of the road, and which are awkwardly located and less likely to attract footfall?

Visiting an area is one thing, but ideally you want to live there so you can witness the changes as they're happening. If you're in residential property, you want to look at the new buyers and renters, and whether they differ from the existing crowd. Even one or two households can give you a sense of which way the wind is blowing. If you're sitting on a property that's worth £100k at the last valuation, and one down the road goes for £150k, then there's a window of opportunity to start buying up at the existing benchmark, with a clear indication of where it's soon going to be.

Most successful people in property are highly focused and specialized. They have their areas, where they know everyone and everything that ever happens, giving them a level of market intelligence and market reputation that enable them to make great deal after great deal. In every town or city you visit, there will be a local property mafia of some sort. If you know your patch and have the capital, then over time you can start to influence it.

Unless you're in an area, sensing the first indicators of how it's changing, you're unlikely to be ahead of the crowd when things break in favour of new investment. That's why being in the estate agency business has served us so well, as a key part of how we understand the property cycle and judge our investments. For a property professional, there is no better way of being on the ground than having a high street presence like that, where you are right in the middle of the flows of people and money, listening every day to the market and hearing what's changing before the market has woken up and responded.

You don't need to be an estate agent to know your patch, but you do need to have that kind of in-depth insight into an area or property sector before you can even consider investing.

Educate yourself – read the news

Market intelligence might sound like it's some great secret, revealed only to the chosen few, but the reality is that it's everywhere. In fact, a large proportion of what you need is widely available on a daily and weekly basis. The information about who's buying and selling, what's coming onto the market and where major investments are about to happen is all there in plain sight.

What are you looking for? It might be a building or portfolio that's coming up for sale; it could be that someone is retiring and closing down their fund (in which case you have a motivated seller and potentially a better price). If you're an investor, scour the pages both for announcements of what's coming onto the market and indications of what soon might be.

You might think that once this information has been published, it's too late to be of any use. But often the opposite is true. Most people walk around with their eyes shut, and they also pick up the trade magazine and put it down without doing anything with what they've learned. Few people actually decide to pick up the phone as a result, introduce themselves and start what could become a profitable negotiation. Once you start hunting down opportunities and realize how readily available they are, you will wonder why more people don't do it.

Sometimes the information you're looking for is obvious, in the form of announcements about who's buying and selling, opening up or closing down. At other times it's more about the indication of how different areas and sectors are doing. You might be looking to invest somewhere where the price has been too high. A struggling high street or a softening market in residential or commercial property could be the signal that the price is going to come down to where you want it to be. Everything you read about your market tells you something and some of it will be intelligence that you can use straight away.

Remember that you're not reading for the sake of it, or because you haven't got anything better to do. All the news that goes into a weekly edition of the *Estates Gazette* or *Property Week* is telling you something about how, and when, to invest or take winnings off the table.

And in today's market, beyond the familiar publications, there are any number of website and social media feeds that allow you to follow the goings-on and market analysis on a daily and hourly basis. Those who educate themselves the most about their market and its fluctuations are always the best placed to know when and where to strike or pull out.

Agent relationships are key – nurture them

What you see going on around you, and what you read in the press, provides a good slice of the market intelligence you need to make good investment decisions. But not everything is in plain sight. Some of the information you will need isn't on the street or in the newspapers, but sits with the people who are the brokers and gatekeepers to the deals you want. In this case, that means property agents.

Agents are the lifeblood of the property industry. In the end, they are generally the ones who present offers to their client and advise them whether or not to accept. You need them on side to make deals, but you should also see them as one of the most important sources of market intelligence.

The truth about any business is that it's people-driven, and that applies as much to bricks and mortar as to any other industry. If something important is going to happen – a major sale, investment or development – then there are agents who will know about it.

Agents are the gatekeepers to information as much as they are to specific deals. If you want the best market intelligence, then you have to get to know them. As a professional that means reading the media they read, hitting the bars they frequent and going to the events where you know they will be. There's a whole community of people who get together to talk about what's happening, the deals they're doing and the rumours they're hearing. If you're not involved in that conversation, then you're missing out on some of the most important intelligence around. What you hear from people who are trying to impress each other – and, yes, here alcohol plays a part – would amaze you. There are no secrets in a business that is fuelled by gossip and relationships. You will find that market intelligence is gladly shared socially.

In the early days I would ring and ring agents so they knew me, and what I was looking for. I went to every event going, and built relationships with people who at that point didn't necessarily want to know me. You have to get stuck in and make yourself a part of that world. In the end, someone is going to present you with a deal. Today, of course, the boot is on the other foot. Agents who once would never have taken a call from me will tender for our business. And we'll host groups of up-and-comers under our own roof. But the forum doesn't matter so much as the nature of the interaction. You need those relationships to build up your market intelligence and to get the inside track on deals and major developments. If you want to swim, you have to be willing to get your feet wet.

If you're not in the industry but looking to make some investments, then the same point applies. Building agent relationships doesn't mean turning up at the head office of Savills and demanding to see the CEO. If you're a prospective residential investor, then go to your local high street estate agency and introduce yourself. Tell them who you are and what you're looking for. Go on a Wednesday (on Friday everyone's busy with completions, while on Mondays they're still shaking off the weekend) and have a chat with the agents there about what they've got on the books. Then go back the next week – and the one after that. By the third week you'll be asking them how their holiday was, and by the fourth how their kid's first day at school went. If you're serious, by the fifth I can all but guarantee they will be presenting you with a deal that you can buy well. It's all about building the relationship and earning your place at the table (by which point, you need to have all your market intelligence in place and your assessment of local valuations down to a tee: agents can offer you deals, but it's your responsibility to know what's a good price).

The agent community is one that's constantly moving and changing, so it's not enough to get to know one or two and hope they can meet all your needs. Most likely, the guy you've been building a rapport with will have disappeared by week four, to another job or another country. Spread your bets and if you're serious, go to every local agency and build a proper network of contacts. Lots of people go and have a chat once, but not many keep on following up. Agents are doing this all the time and know how to separate the window shoppers from real buyers. Show them you're serious, and good things will come your way.

Surround yourself with good advisers

I talked in Chapter 5 about the importance of picking a brilliant team of people to work for you: those who may have more skill and expertise than you do and who can be trusted to run whole parts of the company under your direction. I also mentioned the challenge of selecting professional advisers. But this is one that has to be grasped, because a property investment is not a solo enterprise: it's a transaction that is going to include a range of advisers from surveyors to lawyers and accountants. You need third-party experts, so like everything else they need to be the best available and the most suited to your needs.

Take lawyers. There are property lawyers, and within that category there are people who specialize in residential, commercial, investment and development. And within those niches, there are people who focus on your local area and know all the players. You don't just need 'a' lawyer or any property lawyer: you need someone who is deeply embedded in your sector, and generally your area as well.

Don't just find a good and appropriate lawyer. Build a relationship with them. Conveyancing (preparing the documentation for a property transaction) is an administrative process, and the reality is that it usually takes as long as it takes your lawyer to get around to it. If they don't really know who you are, expect your deal to be well down the pile on their desk. You need to build a rapport, and create a sense of the future business you might do together, to get the quick result you need.

Before you ever get to that stage, you need to know what and who you are investing as. Most people's first instinct is to buy in their own name or through a company. But at that point they don't know if this is going to be a one-off or the beginning of a large portfolio. It doesn't make sense to set yourself up corporately if you're only going to do one or two deals. But equally, if you are serious, then you need the right advice about how to structure the investment vehicle for your investments to maximize your returns. It might be anything from a partnership to a limited company, or an LLP. It could be locally domiciled or held offshore. These are all questions you need to take advice on from a good accountant – again, one who isn't a jack-of-all-trades, but a specialist in the specific arena you have chosen to invest in. Fail to get this right, and what looks like a brilliant return is going to be badly eroded because you've got the company structure wrong and end up paying through the nose in taxes.

A good bench of advisers makes all the difference. These are the people who will likely stay with you over the course of years and decades, creating a mutually beneficial relationship where everyone does well. Having good advisers, those who can help you to conclude transactions efficiently, is also another way of building a good reputation with agents. If an agent knows that a deal always goes smoothly, and quickly, when you're on one end of it, who do you think they are going to bring their next good one to? Always remember you're dealing with people, and that the agent is thinking about how quickly the commission from the sale is going to land in their account. Speed and efficiency are major assets if you can cultivate them as part of your market reputation.

So advisers matter, and you need to choose them early and well. Not sure where to start with that? Then find someone who can help.

This is why every serious property investor should find themselves a mentor. When you're just starting out, and have never done a deal in your own right, there's lots you won't know. So seek out someone who does and who is willing to act as an informal adviser or a more hands-on mentor. I met people who were much more accomplished and sophisticated while sitting on the Chamber of Commerce board. They were the ones who helped recommend the right advisers for me, and from whose companies I learned many of the good business and investment practices I am recommending here.

A mentor can stop you from making bad mistakes, and you will learn plenty just by watching how they go about their work. They show you what the next step up looks like, and what you will need to change to play at their level, or even close to it. Plus, they can help you find a good lawyer.

Don't assume you know everything (you'd be surprised how many first-time investors, even those who know some people with relevant experience, don't get advice about their first deal and end up overpaying because they were too proud to check). Always be prepared to ask for help from those who have been in your shoes and prospered.

It's hard to emphasize enough how important market intelligence and relationships are to successful property investing. It's intelligence that dictates what, where and how you buy; and when it's the time to sell up. It shows you who to talk to if you want to seek out the opportunities that haven't yet come to the market. Much of that intelligence is going to come through investing in your relationships and relentlessly building your network: getting the tips before everyone else does and being offered the deals before they go on the market.

This is an industry where you need your ear constantly to the ground and to be shaking as many influential and well-informed hands as you can. Unless you're scouring the news every day, getting out from behind your desk to survey what's going on in your patch and pressing the flesh with agents, you're going to miss out on all sorts of important events that point the way towards future deals.

You've got to do the hard work to find market intelligence, but once in a blue moon an opportunity is going to fall straight into your lap. Years ago, a guy wandered into one of our high street estate agencies, demanding to see whoever was in charge. From my office at the back, I could hear him being rude to our reception staff and shooting his mouth off about how he was going to buy the properties neighbouring ours, which had just come up for sale. He didn't make it past the front desk, but nor was his intervention ignored. I picked up the phone, talked to the landlord for that bit of the high street, and on discovering the intelligence was good, made an immediate cash offer for the assets. By the time he worked out what had happened, and returned to our office to complain, our offer had been accepted. Which goes to show the importance of guarding the intelligence you hold, as well as seeking out that which you don't.

The need to stay on top of your market intelligence never goes away. I've now got a team of people working for me whose job this is, while potential deals are sent to us every day of the week. But I'm not earning my keep unless I keep sticking to these basic disciplines and reach my own conclusions about where the market is going and how we can take advantage. I pick up the papers and then the phone, just as I did thirty years ago when I had none of this infrastructure around me.

The other point is that I really enjoy doing it. I won't drive down a high street anywhere in the world without clocking the 'To Let' and 'For Sale' boards and forming an instant impression about where the investment opportunities lie. Perhaps I'm cursed and can't help myself, but this is definitely a profession that worms its way into your psyche. There is something almost a bit addictive about it, and there's nothing more exciting than finding a new opportunity and instantly starting to visualize what you could do with it. You should find yourself enjoying this 'hunting' part of the job; and if you don't, perhaps think twice about whether this is what you really want to be doing with your life or your spare capital.

Intelligence and relationships are an essential part of the due diligence needed to source opportunities and identify deals. They get you onto the pitch. But then you have to play. So how do you buy a property, buy it well and realize the maximum return from it?

Buying well and making a profit

You might have expected me to begin this chapter with how to buy. But that is precisely the mistake that far too many people in the property market make. They think buying is the first thing you do. Having just inherited some money, or new to the business, they want to get started straight away. This couldn't be more wrong. Buying is not the beginning. It's the culmination – of all the work done to educate yourself about the market, the area and sector you plan to invest in, and to build relationships. Forget about even trying to invest before you have done all of the things described above. Before this point you don't know enough to know what is and isn't good value, you don't have the right team around you to transact efficiently and you are liable to make the critical error of property investing: getting the entry price wrong.

Don't even think about yourself as a buyer before you've done the work needed to build the right foundations and get your market intelligence up to scratch. Then, and only then, should you approach the market as a serious investor. Even at this point, your work is only just beginning.

Do your homework

I've already talked about the importance of gathering market intelligence, through a combination of window shopping, networking and reading the relevant news. That is about developing a generic level of insight into a sector and specific local market, as well as how the industry works as a whole. You need this to get into the right space in the first place. Getting ready to actually buy requires a whole extra level of due diligence.

One obvious question is how do I find the right properties to invest in? You can use the obvious sources of what's listed on the market or use your agent contacts to see what's about to become available. But often the best deals are for properties that are never made publicly available in the first place. If you know how to look and approach people, potentially every promising piece of real estate you pass in the car or walking down the high street could be your next deal.

If, as has recently happened, I move into a new area and start looking at some of the local high street property, there are a number of steps I'll take to better inform myself about the nature of the property, its value and the possibility of making a deal.

After getting a sense of the area and clocking the flows of supply and demand, the next stage is to find out who owns the building, and if there is an appetite to sell. It's not hard to find out who the landlord of a given property is. Often it will be displayed somewhere in public view, or if not you can ask the shopkeeper or have a lawyer perform the search. You should quickly be able to find out details about the landlord and the managing agent. That gives you a first port of call.

Speaking to the agent will give you a sense of whether a sale is even remotely on the cards. Is it a long-term hold? Often the answer is definitely yes, but sometimes there will be a flicker. They'll say something like 'We could think about it, if the price is right.' A statement like that starts to open up a negotiation. At this point, the next step is to ask for the tenancy schedule.

Once you have that, you know who the occupiers are and what their lease terms are. That is where you can start to make an informed judgement about the valuation. You can see which leases are coming to an end, how the rent stacks up against comparables and whether tenants are financially solvent. All this informs essential judgements such as how you will value your offer and what you plan to do with the property as an owner (whether, that is, to refurbish and raise rents or seek a change of use or planning permission for a redevelopment). At this point the two most important elements – the price you are willing to offer and the plan you create for the investment – start to fall into place.

Next, you need to check that your expectations around price are in the same ballpark as the vendor's. And then you can have a conversation about whether a deal is possible or not. Around half the time it usually is, if you can provide capital certainty and get it done quickly.

Sometimes the best deal is one that you create just by window shopping, finding something that has potential and approaching the vendor as I've described. You have to plant quite a few seeds, only a few of which will actually grow, but the ones that come off turn into deals where you are the only bidder and yours is the only price. Whatever you choose to invest in, homework of this kind is a necessary foundation for any property deal. Know exactly what you are buying, what you are going to do with it once the deal goes through and that you've got the right price.

Buy well – you can't change the entry price

This sounds like an obvious point that is hardly worth pausing for. Except nearly everyone gets it wrong. You wouldn't believe how many people, especially first-timers, blunder in and pay too much to buy a house or flat. This is the fatal error of property investing. If you've paid too much, it's going to be a struggle all the way to make any kind of decent return. You'll be playing catch-up for the whole time you hold the investment.

With any property there are all sorts of things you can change to improve your yield and eventual return. You can change the use, refurbish the interior and swap the tenants. Once you have your hands on it, there are many different tools at your disposal to create value. But the one thing you can never change, once contracts have been exchanged, is the entry price. The fate of any property investment is set at this first stage. The price really does have to be right if the return is going to be what you hoped for.

So how do you buy well and ensure you have got an entry price that can set you up for a serious profit? This is where the market intelligence and network you've spent time building comes into its own. Buying well means that you know your patch down to the last detail, and you've got every possible comparable valuation lined up before weighing your offer. It means having your finger on the pulse of what is changing: when prices are about to go up but there's still an opportunity to get on the elevator before the doors shut. Or it means knowing that a market is in downturn, but being patient for prices to get really cheap and bottom out before you dive in.

Buying well is about being clear-sighted and patient, picking your moment and your target in a market where all the pieces are constantly moving. Owners will flee a market they fear to be sinking – high street retail being a good current example – but that offers an opportunity for buyers who can get good value cheaply. Much of my recent success has been based on acquisitions made at the bottom of the post-2008 market crash, in fundamentally strong properties that recouped their value and delivered substantial profits. Other examples of buying well are when you see an opportunity that others are missing, or pick up on some market intelligence about a new development that is going to have a major bearing on local valuations. Again, it's about knowing the plan for that investment before you exchange, having a clear idea of what your profit is going to look like and buying with the certainty that as an active investor you will reap an impressive return – not just hope to stumble into one as the market rises.

Above all, buying well has to mean you are prepared not to buy at all. Too many people rush into this market with money burning a hole in their pocket, in a hurry to do some deals and make their mark. A desperate buyer is going to end up a poor one. Because if you're rushing, you haven't been through the disciplines I've described to do your homework properly, you haven't developed a network and market intelligence to know the right price, and the vendors and agents will see you coming a mile away.

Of all the things you need to be successful in property investing, the right entry price is the first among equals. Take your time to get this right every time: finding the right deal, and making sure once you have, that you get the appropriate price. The blunt reality is that if you stumble at this point, then you're going to end up flat on your face. If you want to make money in this business, you need to be allergic to overpaying. Be patient, wait for the right opportunity and get the price right.

Secure preferred buyer status

Property is a highly competitive space. Everyone in the market has capital and there are buyers everywhere. You're swimming in shark-infested waters. So how do you win the race? There are a number of different ways to get to the place you need to end up, with the status of preferred buyer.

The most obvious is market reputation. We get deals done now because vendors and agents know that we have guaranteed capital, work quickly and that our money will be in their bank account while another buyer is still scrambling to raise the necessary finance. That's the benefit of having been in the business for over thirty-five years, in which time we have been consistent and fair in our dealings and always delivered in the time frame promised.

Over time you can build a reputation like that and profit from it. But how do you become the preferred buyer when no one knows your name? This comes back to shopping where others aren't. If you're the only purchaser, then by default you become the preferred buyer.

My philosophy has always been straightforward. I don't hunt where everyone else is hunting. While they wanted to buy three-bedroom terrace houses, I was buying the high street. When they then started to buy the high street, I went to the town centre office blocks. When they all started flooding to agents, I tried going direct to fund managers. You should sell to a herd, but never buy as part of one. Demand dictates the prices go up, and it's harder to push your way to the front of the preferred buyer queue.

It's about where you look, so cast your gaze towards the unfancied bits of the market: buildings that have become unloved and even unprofitable, but which with better management, a change of tenant and potentially a change of use could quickly become a good investment. There is a category of property we call the institutional orphan: what was, a decade earlier, a good investment for a property fund, but over time has become less and less attractive as the lease runs down and the requirement for refurbishment goes up. This might be a row of shops or an office block. It doesn't look hugely attractive, but you know there's value in it if you are an active investor who will make the necessary improvements to create value. Most importantly, you can get a good price from a vendor who wants it off their hands, and if you anticipate that need before the fund has put it on the market, you can knock on their door and get there first. Quickly, you go from being a window shopper to a preferred buyer on a property which you can make improvements to and a healthy profit on.

You can also become the preferred buyer by being one of the only people willing to put money on the table in a difficult economy. When the West Bromwich Building Society ran into difficulties during the financial crisis, the agent they had instructed called me because they knew I was one of the only active buyers in the area for the head office they were looking to offload. I bought the building, which I know had been on their books for over £7m pre-crash, for £450,000. The sale of some derelict houses at the back of the property (which came as part of the deal) immediately made that money back. The subsequent sale of the main building gave us an overall seven-figure profit. The only money we had put down was an initial £45,000 deposit on the purchase price.

You increase your chances of becoming the preferred buyer if you are willing to approach organizations you know or think are willing to sell. Once you are in that space, the ability to get a great entry price and do a beneficial deal will follow.

Know your vendor – and find their hot button

Once you've done all your preparations, and potential deals are on your radar, you need to start thinking about your vendor. A lot of property investing is fundamentally a science – working out valuations and yields on the basis of a series of fixed and known factors. But in making deals you need to appreciate the human factor too. Everyone you are dealing with is a person, motivated by the same two things that motivate all of us: fear and greed.

You can't buy well without understanding what the vendor you're buying from is worried about, and having a sense for when their greed is going to kick in. What I always say to my team is that we need to identify the vendor's hot button. Are they about to retire or close their fund and looking to make some quick sales? Are they looking to divest from this sector to reinvest in another? What does the price need to look like for them to get the approval of their shareholders? Whatever it may be, you need a motivated vendor, and you need to understand the nature of that motivation.

This is where your research and market intelligence come into their own. People don't walk around wearing a sandwich board saying 'sale', but you can work out when one's on from a combination of what you read and what the advisory community is telling you. If you're sufficiently plugged in, you'll know when somebody is on the move in a way that might allow you to make some good acquisitions.

Other times, you might read something and follow the trail back to a motivated vendor. I once bought the site of a sixth-form college from a council. It had previously been put up for sale four times and failed to find a buyer. Stories kept appearing in the local press and it was clearly becoming a bit of a running sore. So I rang them up, made an offer that was about a third of what they had initially wanted, and was gladly received. The money might not have been what they were looking for, but by that point the primary motivation was to bring this episode to a close, get the building off their hands and stop the story running in the local press. No vendor will sell to you without some kind of motivation – your job as an investor is to work out what it is and how you can use it in your favour. If someone needs to see the money in their account – and you can transact quickly – then they are going to come down to your price, not hold out and risk losing the deal. These are the situations where you stand to make a substantial profit by securing a highly competitive entry price.

All the same dynamics are there when you deal with agents. Typically you will negotiate with an agent who acts on the vendor's behalf. You are looking to reach a point where the agent will recommend that their client accepts the deal on the table. Remember that agents get paid in commission: if you're talking about a deal and say your price is £2m, as you're on the phone they will probably be scribbling £20,000 on a pad of paper – their 1% commission. Once you get down to the money part, people start mentally allocating it: if the deal goes through they can hit this year's budget, give bonuses, move house. Even among vendors who can be reluctant, the prospect of quickly having the money in their account can be a powerful lure. The same applies to agents: they want a deal to happen, as long as they think it's fair for their client.

Knowing your vendor isn't just about understanding their motivation to sell. It's also about knowing who you like to buy from. If possible I always deal with institutions rather than individuals or family trusts, who can come with complex ownership structures and interpersonal relationships. For institutions it's always just business. Whoever you choose to deal with, don't enter a negotiation without understanding what has brought them to the table, and how you can use that to your advantage to secure the best price – which is always one that leaves both sides satisfied, but you as the purchaser with ample headroom for capital appreciation and profit.

Negotiate hard but fair – always justify your pricing

I'm not a very good negotiator, because I only have one price. That's usually what I tell counterparties once we have got down to business. It's true, after a fashion. I don't barter as you would at a market stall: starting very low and expecting to be dragged up towards the middle. My starting offer is always the price I want and expect to pay, based on a careful valuation of the asset in question. There will always be more fuel in the tank, but there are also alternative deals elsewhere, and if the asking price drifts too far from my own, then I'll switch attention to those instead.

Negotiation is fundamentally the art of keeping your options open, while narrowing down those of your counterparty. If I'm talking to someone who hasn't yet listed their property, I will make clear my price and the reasoning behind it. By all means, they should feel free to put the property on the market if they think they can do better. But if they walk away now and want to come back later, then my price will have changed – and not in their favour. You need to make it clear that you have options and won't simply hang around at their convenience, in case they can find a better offer elsewhere.

It goes without saying that you have to negotiate hard. But it also has to be fair. Don't have the mindset that you are trying to make the other side lose out or to profit at their expense. There is usually a way to ensure that both sides leave the table happy, without in any way undermining your need to buy well, at an entry price that will lock in an eventual profit.

A key part of making property negotiations fair is how you justify your price and the valuation that underpins it. I'll never just tell an agent that this is the price and they can like it or lump it. I will always fill in the context: how we have valued the asset based on a combination of comparables, the condition of the property, the maturity of the tenancies and the existing rental yield.

This kind of justification is important for a number of reasons. For one, it's how you show an agent that your offer is credible: not plucked out of thin air based on what you think you can get away with, but something that has been carefully costed based on the available evidence. It's much harder for a counterparty to dismiss your valuation and offer out of hand if you can demonstrate it is based on firm foundations and objective metrics. (If you are miles apart on pricing and the value of some fundamentals, then there's no point going any further and you should look elsewhere.)

Remember also that the agent you are negotiating with has to take your offer back to their client to get it confirmed. If you have done the analysis for them, that makes it easier for them to recommend that the offer should be accepted. They can get their own surveyors and accountants to test your sums, but if you're credible they will know this is going to produce essentially the same result.

Negotiation is an essential part of good property investing, ensuring you get the appropriate entry price. But the real art is more in valuation, and sticking to your guns, than any psychological arm-wrestling. You should always have options and be willing to walk away if you're not going to get your price or something close to it. Don't get emotionally invested in the notion of 'winning' the negotiation. Set yourself clear parameters about what entry price will deliver a good profit, and if you can't get that then say thanks and move on. In any negotiation, you need room to manoeuvre, and that includes preserving the option to walk away and await a better opportunity (because there is no such thing as a good investment that you paid over the odds for; either the entry price is right or it isn't a good investment).

Finally, don't just treat negotiation as something that begins and ends with the transaction. You have to constantly negotiate across the lifecycle of the investment, with your advisers and contractors. You need to negotiate a good price on the plastering, the carpet fitting and the gas bill as much as you do the entry price. Some contractors will always look to boost their margin, so get multiple quotes for each job, and smoke out those which have clearly been inflated. If you want to maximize your profit, then every transaction that sits within the overall investment has to be negotiated fairly but hard.

Add value: don't be a passive investor

For some investors, it's after a price is agreed and contracts have been exchanged that you start thinking about what to do next. Don't fall into this trap. To be successful you have to add value, and you need a plan in place to do that before even entering into negotiations. You need to be thinking as an active owner before you have even made the acquisition (this is essential to understanding the future value of the property and your projected end profit).

It's possible to make money in property as a passive investor. Generally speaking, if you hold onto your investments, the market will trend upwards over time even taking into account some down years. Anyone who has capital can do that, but by remaining passive you are leaving money on the table, surrendering both future sale value and additional income in the meantime.

A property investment is really what you make of it. The condition and use of the building you acquire is simply the starting point. You need to make changes that reflect where supply and demand in the market are, and the most profitable use for the building you now own. You should treat the new investment as a business in its own right: one that needs its own big picture and has ongoing strategies and fallback plans in case your initial approach doesn't work out.

What might those plans look like? As a residential investor, you have to look at what the market is after. Is there more demand for more bedrooms or more living space? Can the garage take an extension or is there room to add something on top? If it's a large house, would you be better served getting a change of use and converting it into flats? Again, these decisions hang on knowing your patch and gathering market intelligence. You need to go where the market wants you to. But the point of listing these various options is to show that you have them. A house isn't simply one building that has to be let out in its current state, at something approximating the current rent. There are all sorts of ways of adapting and improving the asset.

It's no different with commercial property. One large high street property held by a struggling tenant might be more profitably repurposed as a number of smaller shops which can attract new tenants and spread your risk. A shop or an office block might do better as a restaurant or a bank. You have tricks up your sleeve, from refurbishment to changing the tenants, raising the rents and effecting a change of use. You should know before you exchange contracts what plan you want to put in place, and the others should be held in reserve as alternatives in case of need. Be ready to go the moment you take ownership, with contractors or even new tenants lined up so you can immediately start putting your vision into action. There is no reason to lose time and money if you have done your forward planning properly.

Being an active investor or, should I say, an active asset manager, is how you turn a good purchase into a great one. Do it right, and you will increase your income from the property at the same time as helping to ensure the best possible eventual sale price. The building that currently houses our head office, on Colmore Row in Birmingham, has so far doubled in value during the eight years we have held it. We've achieved that simply by buying well. Upon purchase it was occupied by the accountancy firm PwC on a short-dated letting, so nobody else wanted or could get finance to buy it. We refurbished the building, secured better tenants and gained value appreciation. All very simple things, which goes to show that property can be a straightforward business as long as you put the work in and follow the basic disciplines in the way I've outlined. This process never stops. We are presently securing planning approval to add an extra floor to the top of the building, which will add quality lettable space, increase the income and improve the capital value further. Having paid an entry price of £4m, REI has enjoyed a 10%-plus rental yield, with a capital valuation now in the region of £10m.

It's a misconception to think that property is simply a matter of hunting down good deals and negotiating hard. You're not just a property buyer; you're also going to end up as a seller, and the return you see at that point will reflect how actively and effectively it has been managed in between. Getting the right entry price gives you the flexibility to maximize your returns, but you will only achieve that by following through and becoming an active investor. If you want the valuation of your investment to climb as high and fast as possible, then you first have to add some value to the asset.

Gearing: get the debt ratio right and always have positive cash flow

Because of my background, I have always been risk-averse, a trait exemplified by a reluctance to take on any more debt than is necessary. Some of this is due to in-built caution – inherited from my parents and their generation, for whom debt of any kind beyond a mortgage was out of the question. But regardless of your instincts and upbringing, you need to be careful about your gearing (the ratio of debt to assets) and how much debt you take on, so as to avoid losing your shirt when market conditions change.

I have two golden rules when it comes to debt. The first is that you should only take on debt to fund an investment that will be income-generating. If it's a house, office or shop that is going to deliver rental income, then it's fine to take on some debt as part of the purchase. But if it's a development site or some kind of commercial investment that won't generate an income, I will only buy from cash.

My belief is that, even in a large portfolio, each individual investment should stand alone. You don't want a situation where profitable assets are bailing out loss-makers. If it doesn't make you money, then don't go into debt to buy it. This helps ensure you don't get into the most dangerous situation for a property investor, where you are over-geared and have taken on too much debt to build a portfolio that creates insufficient cash flow. One of the first rules of any business is that it doesn't matter how many assets you hold if you run out of money. A good business can quickly go bad if cash flow dries up. Those who get it horribly wrong in property have usually ended up in a situation where they were asset rich but cash poor. As the banks famously found out in 2008, a lack of liquidity can quickly become fatal when confidence takes a dive.

My second line of defence against becoming too highly geared is to ensure that my bank covenants always exceed my loan-to-value ratio. If we borrow to fund an income-generating asset, that will generally be a loan with an LTV of 50% (i.e. a loan of half the asset's total value). That will be backed up with a bank covenant of 75%, ensuring that even if the market moves against you, the covenant secures you for more than the value of your initial loan.

The other advantage of not over-borrowing is that the bank will give you a better rate and lend you more money across other assets because you're lowly geared, and your risk profile will not be flashing any red lights.

As you build your portfolio, use debt but do so sparingly and think carefully about what it is being used to fund. The situation to avoid, above all others, is one where you end up with a beautiful parade of assets, but insufficient cash flow when the market turns against you and the tide goes out. You need flexibility to ride the ups and downs of the property cycle – and that means retaining a healthy amount of liquidity and not becoming too highly geared.

Manage risk

This cautious approach to gearing is one important way to manage the risk inherent in any property portfolio. At all stages, however, you need to be conscious of the risks of your investments and how to mitigate the threat of a market dive.

Like any other investment category, property is subject to the fluctuations of the market, and any particular area or sector can experience a downturn at short notice. I'll talk more about the nature of this property cycle in the next chapter, and how you can price it into your planning.

The important thing is to be constantly aware that the market can change without notice, and to be ready for it. Maintaining a healthy cash flow and limiting your debt to lowly geared, income-generating assets is all a part of this approach. There are two other key components of risk management in property: a diverse portfolio and regular stress testing.

1. Diversification

One of the worst things you can be in this business is concentrated in any one small area or sector. If I have put all my eggs in high street retail, or I don't have anything except office blocks, then I am fully exposed to the ups and downs of that particular market. If it goes down the pan, then so do I. As with any investment, by diversifying you spread the risk and limit your exposure to the vagaries of any one micro-market.

A property portfolio should be diversified in a number of different ways. You want diversity of property types and diversity of locations, tenants and sectors. This doesn't in any way preclude the need to specialize. You can be, as we are at REI, a specialist investor in commercial property in the Midlands and still have a diverse portfolio. Ours includes everything from care homes to hotels, retail, doctors' surgeries, restaurants and office buildings. Our largest tenant represents approximately 3% of our income. We are well covered against any one sector, location or tenant going south.

You also want diversification in how you bank (we will be working with eight to ten banks at any one time) and on your bench of advisers. Don't get into a situation, in any part of your portfolio or how it is managed, where you are reliant on one person, institution or market segment. Any of these can suffer the commercial equivalent of being hit by a bus at any time. Only by being diversified can you absorb these challenges, as nobody is immune to things going wrong.

2. Stress testing

As well as achieving diversification, you also have to constantly stress test your assumptions and business model, looking at how your portfolio will stand up to a variety of changing market conditions. You should be 'war gaming' how you would respond to a market downturn, and ensuring that any number of possible scenarios won't have a serious impact on your portfolio. This is something our FD will do on a quarterly basis as a matter of course, and which the bank will also want to do as part of the covenants you hold. In addition, we always hold a substantial cash reserve as a rainy day fund, and a pot for acquiring non-income-generating assets, giving us the ability to capitalize on a material market downturn.

Sometimes, you will feel like you're on a roll and that nothing can stop you. There are moments when the market is running hot, in your favour, and it's easy to feel invincible. But as a friend of mine found out some years ago to his cost, you should never let this impression cloud your judgement and forget the need for rigorous risk management. He was running a house-building business, one of the biggest in the Midlands. Before the financial crisis, his main problem was how to keep up with soaring demand. It seemed like the gift that could only keep on giving. The fact the business was heavily geared, and lacked alternative sources of income, didn't seem to bother him. People weren't going to stop buying houses, were they? But of course when the crisis hit, and the banks stopped lending, the torrent of buyers dried up almost completely. Under pressure, the banks, who once loved and queued up for him, called in their loans and that business, with nowhere to go, effectively collapsed. Had the risk management been better – for instance by holding onto some of the houses it was building, securing ongoing rental income and the opportunity to sell later at a significant profit – then the outcome might have been different.

However good things may seem in the moment, remember that nothing lasts forever, every market has a reverse gear and in any property career you will go through difficult periods. If you have got your gearing right, diversified your portfolio and scrutinized the risks facing your business, then you will be fine even when the market temperature drops below freezing. But fail to do these things, and a train that once looked unstoppable will very quickly come off the rails. The property market is littered with those who crashed and burned because they expanded too fast, took on too much debt and paid scant attention to managing risk. You need to be diligent and retain a keen eye for risk and how it can be managed in order to avoid joining that club.

Have a big purchase – and establish the scale of your business

Everything I've described so far is about landing the early deals that get a property business and portfolio started. It's slow work developing the market intelligence, the network and the local knowledge that positions you to buy property well. There is a lot of discipline required in even getting off the ground. But once you have, you need to start looking at what comes next: thinking strategically about how to build your portfolio and reputation.

So far, you've heard me talk a lot about market reputation. This is a deciding factor for any business and something you have to build and protect with care. Your reputation becomes a core currency of how you do deals, providing a certainty that you will deliver on your promises and that you can be trusted to make things happen quickly.

Reputation is slowly built (and just as quickly lost), but in the property industry it's also something that can occasionally progress in big leaps. For any successful investor, one of these will come when you first make a purchase that makes the market around you sit up and take notice. A big deal shows everyone – from your peers to the advisory community – that you are more than just another small-time player. It signifies that you have arrived as something more than an investor who can do a few tidy deals that don't make much of a ripple.

It needs to be an investment that is akin to the man-of-the-match performance in a crunch game for a footballer, or a first hit single for an up-and-coming band. It should make those watching realize they can't afford to ignore you.

For me the first big purchase was probably an unconventional deal I did with the local council, purchasing some undeveloped land they had been struggling to do anything with. I persuaded them to let me have the land for free, in return for a share of the future rental yield. Not long after, I sold on the contract for a multiple six-figure deal. This was in the mid-1990s, and the cheque was so much bigger than anything I'd previously seen that I took a photocopy of it. (In the days when cheques were still common currency, I actually kept a file of those amounting to six or seven figures.)

Do a deal like this – one that's either big or unconventional enough to catch the eye – and it becomes the calling card. Suddenly you're the one who did the McDonalds deal, made that smart turn on the unwanted bit of council land or saw an opportunity that everyone else had missed. It's a sign of your ability to play at the next level and creates immediate reputational capital with those you need to impress: from banks to agents and other investors. And if a big deal isn't immediately in your reach, then you should work hard to establish and promote the scale of your business, showing the market what you are capable of, and attracting the same kind of attention and respect.

With a big purchase behind you, suddenly those who wouldn't take your calls will be trying to get hold of you. Deals that would never have previously crossed your desk start coming your way. People start trying to network with you, when previously you had to make all the running. You've moved up a seat towards the top table.

If your ambition is to become a major-league player in your local property village, then at some point you are going to need a big purchase behind you: something that can turn you from an also-ran into a contender. So once you've done some deals that have turned a profit, given you confidence and begun the process of building a network, start thinking about what your statement purchase might look like. Consider whether and how you can put down more money than you have before, aim higher and secure a bigger fish than has previously seemed possible. Stretch your horizons and work out the most ambitious deal you could do. Then pursue it with everything you've got. On the council deal I've mentioned, for a while they didn't want to know. I wasn't anyone to them, and it took a lot of pursuing and persuading even to get a conversation started. The door to a big purchase doesn't just swing open in front of you. More likely, you will have to hammer it down. But the effort will be worth it. With a major deal on your books, you will have truly arrived.

Be patient!

Someone once approached me after a talk I'd given to an industry group. 'I never realized before,' he said, 'that it takes fifteen years to become an overnight success.'

This is the reality of achieving success in the property world. It's a slow-burn industry where you have to be in it for the long term if you're going to be in it at all. The richest returns come to those who take a patient approach to realizing the maximum value from assets, and building a portfolio that is constantly fuelling its own expansion through regular income and healthy returns.

Every aspect of the property industry demands patience. It takes time and effort to develop the market intelligence and network you will need. It takes time to source the right deals, and you need to be patient, waiting for the right one at the best price. It then takes time for those good deals to come to fruition. There aren't short cuts in any of these stages: you either do all of it or you may as well do none of it.

Of course it's possible to make the occasional quick return. A few years ago, I bought a building for £1.75m on Great Charles Street in Birmingham, and a month or so later someone knocked on my door and offered me £2.5m. Although in some ways I'd rather have held onto it for the long term, a quick and healthy return on that level was too good to turn down.

That is the exception. Never buy something in the expectation you will quickly be able to flip it and make a big profit. Expect to go through the process I have described of adding value and be aware that you will typically have to wait at least a few years before you can consider a sale (though in the meantime, it may well offer a tidy income stream).

If you're someone just starting out in the industry, then I would offer the following as a rough timeline for building a successful portfolio, if you follow the disciplines I have outlined:

Year 1

Focus on networking, market intelligence and getting to know your patch. You might do a deal or two, but don't worry if you haven't.

Years 1–5

Start to do deals based on what you've learned and the contacts you have developed. Build a team around you and focus on developing your market reputation.

Years 5–10

Expand your portfolio, funding the scale of your business with the winnings from the initial deals. At this point you will want to line up your big purchase that makes the market sit up and pay attention.

Years 10+

Into your second decade, you want to be moving from deals for a few houses, or individual commercial property, to bigger lots: multiple purchases and portfolios that corporate and institutions purchasers will find attractive. By this point, your network should be powerful and market reputation starting to do much of the work. Stick it out towards years fifteen and twenty and then, only then, you might just have become an overnight success.

You can't skip a step in this process. You don't build a network or create a reputation out of nothing. You need to build up your pot of credibility and capital through smaller deals you can reach, which eventually allow you to tilt at the big ones. Remember you're not building a house of cards, but a real one that has to be based on firm foundations. The foundations of your property career take time to establish if they are to be done properly and provide an enduring basis for success.

When you've been around this industry for a while, you will have seen all kinds of people and approaches to being successful. There are always newcomers who think they can jump the queue and become major players in a hurry. Sometimes they will make impressive-looking strides, but invariably they're building on sand: a pile of debt rather than the earnings from a thriving portfolio. As quickly as their star has risen, it will fall. Like the runner who sets off the long-distance race too quickly, they cramp up and never make it to the finish line.

Don't be intimidated by those who seem to be racing ahead of you. This is a long game, where the real success stories are investment groups that have been passed down through multiple generations. The longer you keep at it, the more capital and cash flow you build up, creating unstoppable momentum. But that will only happen if you're prepared to show the greatest of all property virtues: patience.

Property is a simple game if you know what you're doing and stick to the disciplines of patience, market intelligence, good entry price, proactive management and risk mitigation. The property market generally goes up over the long term, and for those who can buy and manage well, there are significant returns to be achieved.

But while none of the fundamentals are particularly hard to grasp, it's not an industry for those who are seeking a quick buck or instant fame. A lot of people come in dreaming of yachts and Ferraris, but if you do things properly, you won't be picking up the keys for many years.

If you're prepared to do the hard work, then you will create an investment machine built on outstanding market intelligence, reputation and contacts, one that grows and accumulates capital over time if you continue to treat every next deal with the same care and attention as your first. Don't underestimate the work involved. This is an industry where the path to success is easy to see and understand, but takes relentless stamina, diligence and bravery to actually walk. I've outlined in this chapter the steps you need to take, which apply wherever you choose to invest and in whatever type of property.

Everything I've described will help you to buy property well and make a serious profit from it. But if you are in this for the long term, as you need to be, then it's not just a case of how you buy and sell, but when. Timing is everything, and to prosper sustainably you need to understand the property cycle.

8

The property cycle

When you're going through hell, keep going.
WINSTON CHURCHILL

'What do we do now?' someone said to me in 2008, after the financial crisis had hit. A previously buoyant property market was suddenly in the doldrums: prices had plummeted, capital was running dry and buyers were few and far between.

'Go on holiday for the next three years,' was my response.

The crash of 2008 was the second major economic recession in my career, as it was for most people doing business today. There is only one certainty about the economy, which is that you can be sure it will at some point take a turn for the worse. You don't know when or how bad it's going to be, but you know eventually it's going to happen. And when the economy goes south, generally so does the property market.

If you are going to build a property portfolio for the long term, then you need to understand the nature of these economic and market cycles. You have to be an investor who is sensitive to the first signs of downturn and recovery. Because all the things I've talked about so far – the patient and thorough approach to identifying, buying and managing property – will only pay dividends if you learn how to manage the cycle: buying low and selling high.

The cycle is so important, because it essentially determines whether or not you get the entry price right. Invest at the wrong point in the cycle and you will have got it wrong by default.

Of course everyone would like to sell at the very top, and buy right at the bottom. But no one has timing that good. However, if you are observant and proactive, you can get in near the bottom and sell out towards the peak. As long as you get near enough, you will do very well.

The remarkable thing is that many people invest in property without paying any attention to the cycle at all. They buy when they want to, not at the moment when the market is best placed to be a buyer. This is like trying to walk up an escalator that's travelling downwards. The market always has an essential momentum, and you need to go with the flow if you are to maximize your return.

I first made serious money by divesting my residential holdings before the 1980s bubble burst, before jumping back into the market in the early 1990s. I then got out again in 2006, before the music stopped the following year. On both occasions I had strong cash flow and capital – thanks to a significant portfolio of income-producing assets with low gearing – which positioned me well to capitalize on the downturn along with the additional capital raised from sales.

Now, with institutional money behind us, we have built the £300m portfolio we now hold in the ten or so years since the market bottomed out – taking advantage of low prices and a market where few were buying. This wasn't luck or exceptional intuition: I simply followed the ebbs and flows of the cycle, watching carefully and acting swiftly when I sensed a change. Here's what you need to know about tracking the market, riding the cycle and staying out of trouble.

Everything is an indicator – keep your eyes open

A property market crash never simply happens unannounced. To the majority it will come as a surprise, but if you are watching closely there will always be small indicators of the coming turmoil. Fundamentally, by a cycle we are talking about nothing more than changing levels of confidence, reflected in the readiness of capital and the willingness of buyers and how these affect prices.

There are many ways of tracking these indicators. I've mentioned that our estate agency and auction house businesses have traditionally acted as our main sources of this kind of market intelligence. You know that when the phones aren't ringing so much, lots are hanging around unsold and auction rooms are emptying, a market that had been running hot is starting to cool. Suddenly viewings are tailing off, offers are disappearing and new instructions are no longer coming through the door at the same rate. It's not hard to put the pieces together once these warning lights start flashing.

But you don't need to own businesses like these to have your finger on the market's pulse. You can follow the same flows of supply and demand by scrutinizing the property listings (are the same ones coming up again and again, unsold?), tracking prices and going to auctions yourself. You can look for other tell-tale signs of a slowing market, such as an increase in rentals because people are holding off from buying houses or large reductions in mortgage lending by the banks and building societies.

From my position in the market, there are two other indicators I look for as signs that the market is heading past the point of no return. One is the prices you're being offered. In 2006, I bought an office building in Wolverhampton (tenanted by the now-defunct Carillion) for £4m. Within six months, someone had taken it off my hands for £6.5m. That is too big and too quick a profit for anything other than a market that is overheating significantly. I was delighted to sell up there, but you know that prices like that are too good to be true, and won't last. It was no different in the late 1980s, at the smaller level I was then playing at. Houses I would have bought for £29,950 were suddenly going at around £60,000. Once the valuations start inflating at that rate, you know it's gone too high and everyone is about to take a fall.

You also watch for the disparity between the price of money and the yield from property. In 2006 you had people borrowing at interest rates of about 6–7% to acquire properties that were yielding 3.5–4%. Again, nonsensical behaviour and indicative of a market in which people had started to invest indiscriminately. That happens in part because a property boom attracts investors with no experience, who don't know the first thing about valuations and are desperate to get on the train. Another sign that we were reaching the end of the cycle in 2006 was that our auction rooms started filling up with unfamiliar faces, those I knew not to be part of the local property industry. When the hobbyists are starting to get involved at this level, you know it's become a bandwagon that won't bear the weight much longer. We all know that when you see a bandwagon it is too late!

When a correction or crash is brewing, the market will start showing signs of strain. A combination of slackening demand and skyrocketing prices tells you that the bubble can't inflate any further without bursting. These indicators aren't a closely guarded secret: you need to keep your eyes open, work your contacts and trust your instinct about when prices have become too good to be true.

Divest decisively, re-enter cautiously

If you feel the cycle is about to turn decisively, how do you judge when to sell up and then buy back in? The market is a bit like the weather: you'll see a dark cloud hovering overhead before it starts to rain (though plenty of people simply don't know to look up in the first place). The longer you stay exposed, the greater your winnings stand to be. But leave it a moment too late and you're going to get soaked.

My approach is to make a decisive move out of the market once I have satisfied myself that the indicators are unambiguously showing a market on course for a downturn. When I'm selling brilliantly well but can't find a good entry price anywhere, when I see too many others paying well over the odds and when I drive down the street and keep seeing the same sale and let boards up (often with reduction stickers), then I know it's time to reach for an umbrella.

If you think the market is about to go, then you need to back your instinct and make a decisive run towards cover. We sold out of a lot of property in 2006, when prices had hit what felt like an unsustainably high level, including much of what we had acquired a decade earlier in the recovery from the previous crash. When the rollercoaster is about to dive downwards, it's not the time to hedge your bets and act cautiously. You need to reach a decision about the time to sell and then act as quickly as possible.

If you have got your timing right, you will be selling in what still feels like a boom market. When we divested in 1988 and 2006, economic optimism was at its peak and many thought the good times would never end. You need to have confidence in the fundamental gravity of markets and your own market intelligence about when buoyant demand has stretched prices further than they can bear.

Don't let the fact that others are diving in stop you from following your instinct that it's the time to get out. This is exactly the time to act, while the market is still full of optimists who will meet your asking price. Wait until too many have noticed the raincloud, and you may have missed your moment.

Remember that you don't need to sell at the very top, just close enough to get out at a good price, and take your winnings off the table in advance of the storm to come. Had we waited a few months later to divest in 2006, we could probably have increased our profit even further, but my tendency to need security meant I was happier to be out of the market with time to spare. The later you leave things, the higher the risk that you reach the point where the buyers are no longer there at the price you want.

This is the first part of how to respond to a volatile moment in the cycle. Withdraw decisively from the market to maximize your profits from property you have bought well and to ensure you will be liquid when the market crashes and you want to become a buyer again.

How do you judge the timing of your re-entry? Here, the opposite applies. You need to be cautious and feel your way, testing prices with a deal here and there, working out if and how much further the market might sink. You can't catch a falling knife, so don't get twitchy as the market starts falling. The worst thing you can do here is invest back in too quickly, when prices still have much further to fall. Hence my 'go on holiday' comment in 2008.

My general rule of thumb is that you should wait for prices to reach about half of what they were at the peak of the boom market. You are waiting for the point when confidence has gone, buyers are scarce and weaker owners have gone bust. Only then will prices have reached the low point at which you can do the best deals. This can take time. After the crash of 2007–8, it wasn't until about 2010 that prices bottomed out and the best deals were on the table. (That is not to say you won't pick up exceptional one-off bargains, and your market reputation will help bring these deals to you.)

That was the point when we went to the City and raised institutional money through REI. Even at a capital-scarce moment in the cycle, we had no problem convincing investors who saw the same opportunity we did: to pick up assets with inherent long-term value at depressed prices.

For example, we bought an office building on Colmore Row in Birmingham for £4m at the bottom of the market. Its real value was twice that, which we realized when selling it three years later. But in 2010, the owner had gone into receivership and the bank wanted to realize cash for the asset as quickly as possible. This is the best business address in the city, it was a listed building (which means you don't pay business rates while unoccupied) and there was a brand new skyscraper being built across the road. All the fundamentals of that property meant its value would recover over time. We simply picked the moment to acquire it – when prices were low and the vendor was desperate to sell.

Like it or not, the trough of a downturn is peak time for property investors who have acted carefully and ensured they are well capitalized (through the disciplines described above, especially getting a good entry price every time and managing risk by not taking on unnecessary debt). However much capital you have at your disposal, you need to observe the rhythms of the property cycle and invest accordingly. If you want to make a return on your investment, don't buy at the point that suits you; buy when the cycle is in your favour.

Understand that each property has a cycle

What I've outlined above is an overall approach to riding the property cycle, and achieving the basic aim of buying low and selling high. But unless your portfolio is small, it's unlikely you will be able to divest entirely when a crash comes.

Any market has wheels within wheels, and property is no different. You have to recognize that each asset you own will have its own cycle, and that will be an important part of the decision of when to sell. Although you need to follow the trend of the market, it's not quite as easy as selling everything you've got when the market looks like peaking.

In the previous chapter I talked about the importance of being an active investor, adding value to an asset through a combination of proactive management or development. If you have not yet added the value you have planned – and unless someone is knocking on your door offering an immediate big profit, which does occasionally happen – then it may be worth holding onto the asset through a downturn, to recoup and grow its value over the long term. You will wait longer for the return, but it will rebound all the same if you are doing the right things to create value.

Equally, you may have reasons for selling 'off-cycle': the circumstances of a property may change beyond the point where you can add value by changing the use of the building or making other adjustments. If the geography of a high street changes – say a bus stop is going to be moved – and that means the flow of footfall will adapt with it, your once thriving shop may no longer be looking like such a good investment. When your market intelligence is telling you to sell, then you have to do it regardless of what point in the cycle the market as a whole has reached.

The physicality of a property is another factor you need to take into account. All buildings age and reach a point where they need more comprehensive refurbishment or rebuilding. That part of the cycle also informs the timing of purchase and sale: there are good prices to be had on distressed buildings at any time, if you have the knowledge and confidence that you can unlock value by bringing it back to life.

But overall, if you have managed the cycle right, then you will have bought early enough for your investments to have reached their maturity by the time the cycle is ready to take a turn for the worse.

Just remember that you are not a slave to the property cycle. Part of the nature of being a long-term investor is that you back yourself to add and then recoup value over time, regardless of what the rest of the market is doing. But you need to know what the cycle is, how it operates and how to take advantage of the opportunities it provides to both buy and sell well.

So, what now, and what's going to happen next?

The essential dynamics of a property cycle haven't changed and never will. The basic rhythms of confidence and capital are what dictate the movement of the market. That is why you only really need to look at how people and money are behaving to understand which direction the market is headed in at any given time.

But not everything has remained the same. Government policy and macro-economic conditions affect the nature of the property market, and should inform the decisions you take to protect your interests.

In the first recession of my career, interest rates spiked to almost 15%. That meant cash became the safest of safe havens and we could simply sit on our winnings while the market storm raged. It was a very different story in the aftermath of 2008, when the world's central banks flooded global markets with quantitative easing and relied on rock-bottom interest rates to encourage spending.

We are still living in that era of cheap money, and I believe that will be the most important protection against another property crash in the foreseeable future. The low cost of borrowing is helping guard against the excessive speculation that led to so many going bust in 2008, sinking under piles of debt they couldn't afford.

If there is going to be a financial crisis of some sort, it seems less likely to come from property as was the case last time, and more probably from the asset finance sector. This is another trend that has been fuelled by cheap money, which has funded industry to invest heavily in machinery and plant and, perhaps more significantly, funded consumers to buy cars on hire-purchase deals. Just as indiscriminate lending to borrowers with poor credit histories helped create the property bubble that burst in 2008, the same looks on the cards for asset finance now. Quite simply, you can't make money by giving someone a £50,000 Mercedes and charging them £199 a month. The numbers don't add up, and in the end someone is going to have to take a bath. It's not without reason that most manufacturers are holding their asset finance divisions in separate financial vehicles. But, if that bubble bursts, don't expect it to be another full-blown crisis. This is a much smaller market than property, in a world where the banks are much more heavily capitalized. Both those factors should help to soften the blow when it comes.

In the property market, low interest rates are having something of a deadening effect: organic growth is low, which puts a premium on adding value to a property and creating your own growth as an active investor. While we remain in a cheap money world, neither a wholesale property crash nor a boom is on the cards. As ever, different sectors of the market will proceed at different paces. There is growth in residential, primarily outside of London, for simple supply-and-demand reasons, and supported by both the cheap lending available and the various government schemes that incentivize first-time buyers. You only have to look at the profits of housebuilders to see which way this market is headed. That said, the government needs to sort out the stamp duty mess it has created, and which is preventing many who want to buy from doing so, harming in the process the many industries that depend on homebuying and moving. Expect a managed retreat or a compensatory measure such as a higher rate on foreign nationals purchasing property in the UK.

By contrast, industrial property is grossly overvalued. The office market shouldn't change much, though the product needs to improve with offices more like hotels, featuring gyms, restaurants and better amenities all round. It's likely that there will be an exchange of shorter, more flexible lease terms in return for companies paying a bit more.

In the context of a market that is neither booming nor looking set for a bust, I believe there are two things that any UK property investor needs to understand about what the next decade likely holds, and which are probably underestimated by the majority. They are the future of the high street and the rebalancing of the economy away from London. Let me finish this chapter by discussing each in turn, and highlighting why I believe they will be core to many investment strategies.

1. The high street won't die: it will evolve and thrive

After housing, the high street sector has attracted most public awareness and dominated the property debate. Since the last recession, the constant refrain has been that the high street is dying and will never return to its former glories. The idealized, sepia-tinted images of the butcher, the baker and the candlestick maker are conjured up as evidence for the retail world we have lost.

Superficially, there is evidence to back up this claim. Shop vacancies have been high and a whole variety of retail sectors from booksellers to travel agents and latterly restaurants have suffered from a combination of the internet eating into their business models and too much competition in their market. Some big brands – from Woolworths near the beginning of the recession to House of Fraser a decade later – have hit the buffers, and there will be more to come. Even some of the beneficiaries of the first wave of vacancies – the one-pound retailers and the betting shops – have faced struggles of their own.

It's a grim picture if that's what you want to paint. And there's no denying that high streets are going through a moment of painful change. But the truth is that the high street has never stopped changing, and the idea that there was a static golden age is nothing more than empty nostalgia. The high street has always been a much more fluid entity than many appreciate. As technology and consumer habits shift, it quickly reorganizes itself to meet them. The now ubiquitous coffee shops may feel like they have been around forever, but the first Starbucks in the UK didn't open until 1998. Similarly, the time span between the first Blockbuster store opening in the UK and the last one closing was less than twenty-five years. Local retail has always chased trends out of necessity: it shapes itself around consumer demand, itself an endlessly flexible beast. The high street cycle is much faster and more volatile than the nostalgists ever allow.

It's also a big mistake to think that there is nothing people will need or want from their local high street, simply because they can now do a lot of their shopping online. The coffee shop boom has been one sign that there is a shift from retail to venues where people can come together and spend time, while the convenience imperative will continue driving the shape of future openings. Booming sectors like budget gyms want to get closer to their customers; there will always be a need for places you can nip round the corner to get a pint of milk; and even the geniuses of Silicon Valley haven't yet come up with a way for the internet to cut your hair or give you a beauty treatment. The high street will become more about 'experialism' than materialism, but demand for good high street locations will remain.

We also need to look at the reality of how e-commerce is going to develop and the relationship between online and traditional shopping. It's true that bank branches are closing at a rate of knots, but take note that the UK's main challenger bank, Metro Bank, is opening them all over the place. Even as more customers transact digitally, there will still be a place for physical retail in delivering good customer service. In parallel, even e-commerce brands are now looking towards the high street (consider Amazon's acquisition of Whole Foods and the opening of its first bricks-and-mortar bookstores), understanding that even if people want to buy online, having a high street presence can be an important marketing and customer engagement tool.

That is not to say that every shop that closes is going to be replaced. There will be less traditional retail on the high streets of the future than many of us knew growing up. But that is still prime property, and there are other uses for it. In particular, there is a growing realization that unoccupied high street real estate can play a role in addressing the housing shortage, and be converted for residential use. That in turn will bring more people close to the retail that remains, boosting the lot of those who increasingly see their role as places for people to gather: from the cafes and coffee shops to booksellers.

The high street will always have a role and that will change over time as it always has. Much of that property remains a good investment regardless of this change. Recently, I was approached by a major fund who want to get out of high street retail in its entirety. I was happy to bite their hand off. I think they will be back a few years down the line, paying much more than they sold for. When this market bottoms out, there are going to be some brilliant deals to be made.

2. The UK will diversify beyond London

Although I grew up in London, I have spent my whole career, and built my entire property portfolio, in the Midlands. So you would expect me to say this, but it doesn't make it any less true. The London-centric version of the economy that has been the norm for so long is going to give way to a more balanced picture in the years and decades ahead. Power and capital will diversify towards the regions.

Why am I so confident? You only have to look around you, whether it's Birmingham, Manchester or Leeds, to see that investment is booming. On my doorstep, we've had HSBC and HMRC locate their head offices here, Greater Manchester now plays host to the lion's share of the BBC, and Channel 4 is moving to Leeds. These are the sort of symbolic moves that will bring many more with them, as supply chains grow around new industries. Industry and universities are also starting to march forward hand in hand, investing in R&D and training young people for the jobs of the future. The work that Jaguar Land Rover has done with the University of Birmingham on advanced manufacturing is just one example. Infrastructure is belatedly being put in place too: HS2 will put Birmingham – which for too long thought of itself in opposition to London – into the ambit of the capital and its wider economy.

There is much for inward investors to like about the UK's other great cities. There is more space, better value and access to a younger workforce, with Birmingham having one of the youngest urban populations in Europe. London will clearly remain the central hub for investment, but more capital is going to find its way to thriving regional cities that allow it the room to breathe.

There have been false dawns before, but this time I believe it is different because the political will and leadership exists to turn the potential into long-term success. On a national level, governments of all stripes realize that they can no longer simply focus on London and hope the benefits will trickle down. Sharing the cake beyond London has already started to become a political priority, and that tendency is going to continue over time. The vote to leave the EU was another wake-up call for our South East and London-centric politics, making public representatives think harder about what they need to do to win provincial votes.

At a regional level, we at last have co-ordinated leadership in the form of metro mayors. The West Midlands has one of the most high-profile, the former John Lewis boss Andy Street. He has already done good work to attract investment and attention, including winning host city status for the 2022 Commonwealth Games for Birmingham. He would be the first to admit that his hard work builds on that of the many people who have been making things happen in the region over the preceding years and decades. These are the people you rarely hear about, but whose influence has been considerable. They include leaders of the local business community such as Digby Jones, John Crabtree and Jerry Blackett; those who have driven the culture and tourism agenda like Anita Bhalla and Neil Rami; and educationalists including

Dame Christine Braddock. The combined work of these people, and many others like them, has helped get Birmingham out of the doldrums it entered when industry started to die out in the 1970s – something that had a decades-long legacy. Recall the closure of the MG Rover plant at Longbridge in 2005, a factory that had at its peak employed 25,000 people. The old jobs are never coming back, but at last the city and wider region can look forward to better prospects ahead.

I say all this not simply to bang the drum for my city, but because it's a reality that investors in UK property need to get comfortable with. There's a reason that prices have been growing across much of the country while they have fallen in London. For years, the capital was the only show in town if you wanted to chase the fastest price inflation. That's no longer the case – and as the political system starts to put a premium on the regions, and inward investment buoys up cities outside of London, the opportunities will become more widely spread. As I've discussed at length, location is not everything, but the political cycle is part of the property cycle I have outlined in this chapter – and for the foreseeable future, it is trending away from London. Investors should take note.

Just as everything you do in life should be moving you towards your big picture, every move and deal you make in the property world has a context. You're not just doing one deal; you're building a portfolio. And you're not sourcing opportunities and making investments in isolation: they're all part of a market whose fluctuations are one of the key determinants of long-term profit.

The property cycle – and all of the cycles within it – provides the essential context for all of your investment activities. Just as a farmer or gardener follows the rhythms of the seasons, an investor has to develop an intuitive sense for the movement of the market. Every deal you consider needs to be weighed up in the context of all the cycles it is a part of: the cycle of the individual property, of the sector and geography it sits in and of the wider property market and economy as a whole.

The cycle doesn't have to dictate the timing of when to invest and sell up, but it undoubtedly points the way towards significant opportunities and major pitfalls. Don't make a decision without thinking hard about these cycles and where your investments sit within them. Price all of this into your calculations about valuation, Day 1 profit and ultimate return, and use it to ensure you are getting the golden ticket of a good entry price. Just as you have to know your patch and the people in it, you need to understand the property cycle to get a good deal. Don't spin the wheel on timing: study the market and let its behaviour guide your hand in choosing when to be brave and when to find cover.

Conclusion: make a habit of success

Have more than you show, and speak less than you know.
WILLIAM SHAKESPEARE, *KING LEAR*

At its simplest, life is about the accumulation of habits. Punctuality is a habit. Winning is a habit. Politeness, honesty, attention to detail, patience, positivity, hard work: all are habits that can be learned and honed. And, by definition, the same is true of their opposites.

We follow routines in every part of our life, and those either direct us towards success or away from it. As the American author and entrepreneur Jim Rohn said, '**Motivation will get you started and habit is what keeps you going.**'

Everything I have talked about in this book is fundamentally about how you can develop good habits that will allow you to be successful in whatever field you choose.

It all starts with establishing a big picture that will guide the course of your life and career. Only the accumulation of good habits will enable you to fulfil the promise of that ambition. If you want to be successful, then you have to focus on honing these and cleaving to the disciplines I have outlined in this book. There is no such thing as a person who is punctual, careful, considerate and relentless in their professional life; and late, slapdash, rude and lazy the rest of the time. How you do anything in life is how you do everything. So unless you are prepared to develop good habits that inform every part of your routine, you are not going to be successful.

This is so important because of the nature of success, which is long term, demands patience and relies on constant repetition of good disciplines and techniques. You can't work hard for a few years and expect to live off that. You will only prosper sustainably if the things I have talked about are adopted as habits that carry you through the entirety of your life.

People don't succeed by chance, and they don't fail by accident. Success arises not through coincidence, but diligent and determined application. The recipe is simple, but because the most important ingredient is time, most people lose patience or quit before it is close to being done.

All the advice I have offered in this book is necessary for success in business, property and your life. You need to put in the consistent hard work that will allow you to acquire market intelligence, build a network and become an expert on your patch, whatever that may be. You need to have the fallback plans, to build a brilliant team of employees and advisers and to share the cake with them. In property, you need to get your entry price right, take on debt wisely, plan proactively and always add value as an investor. In any field of business, it is really about what you know, who you know and how you are known. Intelligence, contacts and reputation are the chips you play with, and you have to keep growing your pile over time.

This is all necessary but not sufficient to achieve the success you seek. That can only come if you learn to behave the way successful people behave: showing the patience, the discipline, the relentlessness and the positivity that they exhibit. Success, too, is a habit: one that rests on the development of all the others. Technique is essential to getting things right, but it relies upon a way of life that is geared around achieving the big picture you have set for yourself. What I have talked about in this book cannot be approached on a whim, or as a hobby. It's everything or it's nothing.

That makes being successful sound like hard work, and it is. Whatever your big picture may be, it is going to take decades to achieve if it is something really worthy of your time and effort. There will be many milestones along the way that give you fulfilment, but if the big picture is strong enough it will keep you carrying on towards the ultimate aim. You will have to be relentless.

But the good news is that anyone can do the things I have talked about. If you give yourself permission to aim high and accept the necessity of digging deep into your resources of stamina and determination, then success is there to be achieved. The final thing to remember is that the only definition of success that matters is yours. Don't let anyone else tell you what to aspire to. Set your own terms and don't allow yourself to be told otherwise. Do it your way.

Good luck. It's a long road, but an incredibly fulfilling journey. After all these years, I still feel like mine is only halfway done. There's still a way to go to reach my 101st birthday. It's a Wednesday night, I'll see you there.

QUOTES FROM
BRICK BY BRICK

'Whether you think you can, or you think you can't, you're right.'

HENRY FORD

'The true meaning of life is to plant trees; under whose shade you do not expect to sit.'

NELSON HENDERSON

'There's nothing difficult, or mysterious, about success.'

PAUL BASSI CBE

'No man is a success unto himself.'

UNKNOWN

'It's not about being the best. It's about doing your best.'

PAUL BASSI CBE

'Make real what you make believe.'

JAG SHOKER

'Success is determined by desire and attitude, not ability.'

PAUL BASSI CBE

'What the mind can conceive and believe, the mind can achieve.'

NAPOLEON HILL

'Don't be the man who talks about the man; be the man the man talks about.'

PAUL BASSI CBE

'Go big or go home.'

UNKNOWN

'You'll worry less about what people think of you when you realise how seldom they do.'

OLIN MILLER

'Success is relative: it's about you, not the other guy or girl.'

PAUL BASSI CBE

'The superior man is modest in his speech, but exceeds in his actions.'

CONFUCIUS

'Lose a few battles to win the war.'

PAUL BASSI CBE

'If you see a bandwagon coming, it's too late.'

JAMES GOLDSMITH

'You should never waste a crisis.'

PAUL BASSI CBE

'It's all about the big picture. Don't be afraid to think big and Learn to dream.'

PAUL BASSI CBE

'Never settle, create the life you deserve to live and help others do the same.'

PAUL BASSI CBE

'Life begins at the end of your comfort zone.'

NEALE DONALD WALSCH

'If I'd had some set idea of a finish line, don't you think I would have crossed it years ago?'

BILL GATES

'The more I practise, the luckier I seem to get.'

GARY PLAYER

'There are no limits other than the ones we impose on ourselves.'

DR WALTER BISHOP

'If you fail to plan, you are planning to fail.'

BENJAMIN FRANKLIN

'Have patience. All things are difficult before they become easy.'

THOMAS FULLER

'The price of success is hard work.'

VINCE LOMBARDI

'If you want to go fast, go alone, if you want to go far, go together.'

AFRICAN PROVERB

'Poor thinkers will never be rich.'

UNKNOWN

'Money is a by-product of success. Strive for success and never chase money.'

PAUL BASSI CBE

'If you don't make time for exercise, you'll probably have to make time for illness.'

ROBIN SHARMA

'A wise person should have money in their head, but not in their heart.'

JONATHAN SWIFT

'With great wealth comes great responsibility.'

BILL GATES

'The man who dies . . . rich, dies disgraced.'

ANDREW CARNEGIE

'Do what is right, not what is easy, nor what is popular.'

ROY T. BENNETT

'You need to work out the why: your motivation to succeed.'

PAUL BASSI CBE

'When you're going through hell, keep going.'

WINSTON CHURCHILL

'Have more than you show, and speak less than you know.'

WILLIAM SHAKESPEARE, *King Lear*

'Motivation will get you started and habit is what keeps you going.'

JIM ROHN

READING LIST

Title	Author	Read
Think and Grow Rich	Napoleon Hill	
The Spirit of Success	Norman Drummond	
Body Language	Allan Pease	
Good to Great	Jim Collins	
The Monk who Sold his Ferrari	Robin Sharma	
One Minute Manager	Kenneth Blanchard and Spencer Johnson	
The Art of the Deal	Donald Trump	
The Wisdom of Business	Eugene Weber	
The Rules of Wealth	Richard Templar	
The Richest Man in Babylon	George S. Clason	
Who Moved My Cheese?	Dr. Spencer Johnson	
Rich Dad, Poor Dad	Robert Kiyosaki	
Built to Last	Jim Collins	
How the Mighty Fall	Jim Collins	
Steve Jobs	Walter Isaacson	
What they Don't Teach you at Harvard Business School	Mark H. McCormack	
Outliers	Malcolm Gladwell	
Great by Choice	Jim Collins	

Title	Author	Read
The Miracle Morning	Hal Elrod	
The 100 Year Lifestyle	Dr Eric Plasker	
How to Win Friends & Influence People	Dale Carnegie	
The Prince	Niccolo Machiavelli	
The Millionaire Next Door	Thomas J. Stanley and William D. Drake	
Sun Tzu – The Art of War for Executives	Donald Krausse	
The Secret	Rhonda Byrne	
The Life Changing Magic of Not Giving a F**k	Sarah Knight	
Thrive	Arianna Huffington	
The Laws of Lifetime Growth	Dan Sullivan and Catherine Nomura	
You Will Thrive	Jag Shoker	
Damaged Goods: The Inside Story of Sir Philip Green	Oliver Shah	
The Five Dysfunctions of a Team	Patrick M. Lencioni	
Titan: The Life of John D. Rockefeller, Sr	Ron Chernow	

INDEX